CONTENT IS KING

The Complete Guide to Writing Website Content That Sells

- Grow Your Audience
- Learn SEO Strategies
- Convert Sales

Laura Briggs

Entrepreneur Press®

Entrepreneur Books, Publisher
Cover Design: Andrew Welyczko
Production and Composition: Eliot House Productions

This publication is designed to provide accurate and authoritative information in regard
to the subject matter covered. It is sold with the understanding that the publisher is not
engaged in rendering legal, accounting, or other professional services. If legal advice or
other expert assistance is required, the services of a competent professional person should
be sought.

Entrepreneur Media* is a registered trademark of Entrepreneur Media, Inc.

Library of Congress Cataloging-in-Publication Data
Names: Pennington Briggs, Laura, author.
Title: Content is king: the complete guide to writing website content that sells /
  by Laura Briggs.
Description: Irvine: Entrepreneur Press, [2023] | Includes index. | Summary:
  "The go-to book for crafting a highly-converting website that speaks to your target audience clearly, showcases your unique brand offerings, and distinguishes
  companies from their competition. Uncover winning strategies for writing and
  evaluating your website copy from a professional freelance writer and get ready to
  unlock new opportunities and revenue"—Provided by publisher.
Identifiers: LCCN 2022048286 (print) | LCCN 2022048287 (ebook) |
  ISBN 9781642011173 (trade paperback) | ISBN 9781613084687 (epub) Subjects:
  LCSH: Internet marketing. | Internet advertising. | Advertising copy.
  | Web sites—Design.
Classification: LCC HF5415.1265.P46 2023 (print) | LCC HF5415.1265 (ebook) |
  DDC 658.8/72—dc23/eng/20221019
LC record available at https://lccn.loc.gov/2022048286
LC ebook record available at https://lccn.loc.gov/2022048287

Printed in the United States of America

26 25 24 23   10 9 8 7 6 5 4 3 2 1

For Carol/Mom
Thanks for always backing me.

Contents

PART II
Content Marketing Strategy

CHAPTER 7
SEO: Optimizing Website Content 85

CHAPTER 8
From Website to Content Marketing Strategy ... 103

CHAPTER 9
Blogging Basics 113

CHAPTER 10
Advanced Blogging..............................127

Introduction

Content is king. We're living in a digital age that produces more words and published website pages each day than any person could hope to read. The indexed web contains over 5.99 billion pages of material and content. Over 91 percent of B2B marketers rely on content marketing to reach customers, and 86 percent of B2C businesses think content marketing is a key strategy to reach business goals. Clearly, website copywriting is important, but most businesses and their freelance writers take their best guess rather than relying on proven strategies.

Even as website copywriting grows, many website creators and content marketers are stuck on how to start the process and on writing meaningful content that draws in search engine traffic and creates an instant connection with readers.

CONTENT IS KING

Too many businesses don't have a defined strategy for writing and posting on their websites. Too many new freelance writers don't understand how to map out content for a variety of clients. This book, chock-full of information about aligning content production with best practices, will help both business owners and freelance writers unlock opportunities and revenue.

Content Is King: The Complete Guide to Writing Web Content That Sells helps solopreneurs, those new to content marketing, and freelance content writers uncover the secrets of writing compelling, search-engine-friendly content. As a freelance writer, I quickly learned I couldn't rely on companies giving me fully scoped briefs to create their website content or blogs for them. Many of them had no clue how to get started, pick topics, or feel confident that they had covered all their bases.

Since 2012, I've helped over 400 business owners craft their website copy and content marketing strategies to reach and connect with their ideal audience. From solopreneurs to Fortune 500 companies, every business needs a content marketing strategy and website copy plan. This book is designed to help you cut through the noise and rely on strategies that capture and share your unique voice with current and prospective readers and followers. Having seen where most businesses and freelance writers get stuck, I know what it takes to write outstanding website content that reaches both readers and search engines.

You know you need standout content. While plenty of blogs out there cover the general process of creating content, there's no go-to guide to help freelance writers, journalists, or business owners understand what makes writing for the web different.

This book is a proven path and soup-to-nuts explanation of the most common website pages needed today and how to approach each one for maximum return on content investment.

This book is for:

- Students and professionals looking to improve their digital marketing and content writing knowledge
- In-house and freelance marketing experts looking to help companies create their websites

- Solopreneurs, tech companies, and small business owners who want to launch a company but are stumped on how to tell their story
- Freelance writers or journalists looking to branch out into a new service offering

Here's what you'll find in this book to help you with your content writing journey. I encourage you to read it from beginning to end so that you create a holistic and meaningful website writing strategy, but I also share this here in case you're looking to navigate to something specific.

This book is made up of two distinct parts. The goal of the first six chapters is to help you get the basic pages of your website up. Following that, in Chapters 7 through 12, you'll learn how to develop a content marketing strategy using your existing website as the base. If that second part feels overwhelming, focus on completing the website for now and come back to the other ideas later. Each chapter ends with a short list of concrete takeaways and action steps from the chapter.

In Part I, you will learn:

- Why you need a website and the importance of storytelling
- Basic website architecture, essential website pages, and a bit about site design
- How to create and refine your company's unique value proposition, so you can connect with readers quickly and authentically
- Best practices of writing copy and creating editorial brand guidelines
- The journey your potential buyer takes on the way to becoming your client or customer
- How to outline and draft copy for your site

Then, in Part II, we'll cover:

- Search engine optimization (SEO), which is how you'll help readers find your website
- How to build a content market strategy from your new website
- The basics of blogging as part of your content marketing strategy
- More complex blogging techniques that connect with readers

- ✐ Landing pages, sales pages, and case studies, which encourage your audience to take action
- ✐ When and how to outsource the writing of your website content

How to Use This Book

As I mentioned earlier, I encourage you to read this entire book from start to finish, even if you're planning to outsource your content writing projects to an in-house employee or a freelance writer. This book is designed to teach you what you need to know to either write your website copy yourself or to hand it over to an expert with the knowledge you need to guide and review their work. Part I will help you plan and build a basic website. When you're ready to create a content marketing strategy in connection with your site, use Part II.

The prospect of writing a website can be overwhelming, but here's an example of how you can break down what you learn in this book to get your website copy written and published in just four weeks:

Week 1: Define your purpose, discover mistakes, define your brand story overall, understand how design influences copy, discover your customer's unique voice, and learn examples of brand values companies can use.

Week 2: Determine your brand voice, editorial guidelines, and UVP. Create your website roadmap.

Week 3: Outline and draft your website content.

Week 4: Edit your content, and determine your content strategy for future content.

The need for content is high and is only expected to continue growing in coming years. Having a website is key for any new or established business to reach customers, many of whom begin their search from a device in their pocket. This book will provide the tools you need to outline and draft your own website copy that connects with readers and allows you to grow your business.

PART I

PREPARE, PLAN, AND WRITE

CHAPTER 1

Website Writing 101

A website can be as simple as an online business card that serves to share more information with your target audience. It can also be as complex as your entire digital marketing engine, doing everything from driving organic traffic to email opt-ins and even sales on one platform.

To create a compelling website, you can't ignore the words on the pages. Companies often invest thousands of dollars in the design of their website, and for good reason—bad design can send viewers clicking away faster than they got there. But the other side of effectively using a website for your online marketing strategy is that you can't ignore website content or view it as an afterthought. It's crucial to tell the reader who you are and where you fit into the bigger industry.

When websites first emerged as a digital marketing tool, their functionality was limited. Today, an individual or a company can launch a professional-looking website quickly. But that increased competition means every business has to stand out from the crowd. Because so many people turn to the internet to get answers to their questions, content marketing and website copy must work hand in hand, not just to provide information but also to form meaningful business relationships with your readers quickly and effectively.

How Do You Know You Need a Website?

First of all, you picked up this book! Either you have questions about making your existing website content more functional or you want to cover your content bases in the site you're planning to launch.

Some companies thrive without a website. I write this as a freelance writer who crafted website content for hundreds of law firms, digital marketing agencies, and other businesses for several years without having a website myself.

Maybe you've been getting by with just a strong social media following. That's a great start. But a website is property you own. Staking your claim elsewhere means you could potentially lose all your hard work if any of those social media companies shut down, decrease their viewership or membership, or cancel or block your account. If your Facebook ad account is the core of your marketing strategy, for instance, you'd be completely exposed if your account was suddenly strapped down.

Launching a business that is reliant on another company's traffic source is known as digital sharecropping. It may seem like a good idea, but the number of factors outside your control can expose you to unnecessary risks that could derail your business. On the flip side, owning your email list and your website gives you the opportunity to collect and analyze data while growing your audience. This has both short-term and long-term benefits for you, because it puts you in the driver's seat of your marketing strategy.

More Benefits of Having a Website

A professionally designed, properly optimized website can be a brand differentiator and a sales booster for your company. A website can seem like a massive project, especially for a company or a solopreneur without writing experience, but advanced tech, automation, and the way modern people search for solutions to their problems means you really ought to take your company online.

Digitally advanced small businesses stand to gain a great deal of ground in the coming years. They often experience higher revenue growth, earn at least twice as much revenue per employee, and were much more likely to create jobs over the previous year than their competitors.

Top Reasons to Create a Website
Make Your Business Accessible

Many consumers prefer an accessible business that can be reached whenever it is convenient for them. You don't necessarily need a 24/7 chat feature on your website, but you do need a web presence that meets your clients where they are when it is convenient for them. A website makes you official on a 24/7 basis.

Increase Your Brand Credibility

Over 30 percent of customers don't even consider working with a business that doesn't have a website. Many believe that by having a website, you have made an investment in your company's future. It greatly increases your brand's credibility and makes it easier to attract ideal customers. Without a website, your consumers' questions will center on why you don't have one.

Connect More Authentically With Your Customers

A website can help you tell your brand story and form long-lasting relationships with your clients. Giving your customers a positive user experience establishes trust. The website user experience might be their first interaction with your brand, and a great website experience sets an excellent baseline for future relationships.

Showcase Your Services and Products Your Way

On your website, you get to tell your story your way. You don't have to rely on nondigital advertising options. This is especially important when every customer matters. Showcasing your expertise in a way that aligns specifically with you helps get your message out to the right people and positions you as an authority. You can use website content to help tell your story and connect with your users easily and professionally.

Better Brand Visibility

It doesn't matter how successful or wonderful your product or service is. If no one knows about it, your product or service is unlikely to sustain the business.

Companies use their online presence in different ways. A big company that has been around for decades or has a huge social media following doesn't need a website to get their name out there. They might not need a comprehensive content marketing strategy.

Many companies develop comprehensive content marketing plans to determine how they'll reach their audience, what content they'll use to do it, and how often they'll post to reach that audience. Every business, however, might not need the same kind of content marketing plan. A hairstylist might rely on content shared over Instagram as a visual sample of their work, while a software company might go all in on creating comprehensive guides and how-to articles.

A big food brand, for example, might use their website mostly to provide helpful information to their prospective readers. That helpful information might include their company's history and ethical practices, links to coupons, brand information and ingredients, and their impact efforts. A huge corporation doesn't need content marketing to draw in customers the way a newer business might. We see their name in stores, and it's a brand and set of products most of us have known about for years.

Without the decades of experience in advertising and product placement of a huge company, smaller or newer companies use their websites not just to share who they are and what they do but to provide answers to prospective customers' questions.

Better Search Engine Traffic

These days, you've got to be optimized for Google and other search engines to capture traffic. The way people think about finding companies often leads them to a Google search.

Customers and clients prefer doing their own research to identify who you are and what you have to offer. You can also expect they'll be directly comparing you to your competitors throughout that process. If you have done the right SEO work on your website, you should consistently rank in Google searches for your chosen keywords.

Your Website Is the Base for Your Online Marketing Strategy

Not only can you strategically target your customers and drive the right search traffic to your site, your website can also be the home for your entire online marketing strategy. People might engage with your brand in multiple ways, such as sending direct messages on social media or through your email newsletter, but the one place that can and should be consistent throughout your online marketing strategy is your website. All your traffic will end up there. We'll go into more detail on online marketing strategy in future chapters.

Why Is Website Optimization So Important?

Modern online viewers require their interest to be piqued within a few seconds. Because readers are bombarded with information and advertising, they are selective about the content they consume. They want easy-to-navigate websites with clean designs and visual elements throughout. Considering those factors as you plan your site can make it a great resource for potential customers and clients.

CONTENT IS KING

Let's dig in to how modern readers look for, click on, and scan through websites to better explain why the words on these sites matter.

To get the most out of this book, I encourage you to think like a website reader. What makes you likely to stay on or leave a website? What are your pet peeves when looking for an answer online? For the websites, podcasts, social media feeds, and blogs you follow regularly, what is it about them and their content that continuously captures your attention? The more you can tap into the experiences of your reader and think like one yourself, the easier it is to get your content set up initially. From there, you can test and adjust as needed.

Let's start by covering what you *shouldn't* do with your website content because it can cause a disconnect with readers.

The biggest mistakes companies make when it comes to website content include the following:

- No content at all or very sparse content throughout the site.
- Company-focused content. If you're too focused on yourself and what you see as the biggest reasons they should work with you, this can come across as too promotional and drive readers away.
- Not providing relevant answers to the questions of target customers.
- Using the wrong terminology to reflect the size of your business. If you are a 17-person team, using the term *we* is acceptable. But if you are a solopreneur working as a business coach or real estate agent, write from the personal *I*. That means updating your contact form to say "contact me" or "I am here to help you." The wrong pronouns can create an unnecessary wall between you and your prospective customers.
- Writing lengthier content than needed. Keep things brief and strive to reach the point as concisely as possible. Too many words can overwhelm your readers or even make them feel as though you are talking down to them.
- Getting the design aspect of the site done professionally but overlooking the importance of getting good copy to match.
- Assuming the content just needs to get done and having someone without writing experience or a digital marketing background create it.

⚐ Content that is so generic it can't be differentiated from competitors' content.

If you can avoid these kinds of mistakes, you can focus on building content aligned with your followers' most important needs and positioning yourself as an authority in your niche.

When it comes to drafting your website content, keep two key things in mind: keep it conversational and leverage the power of storytelling.

The Power of Conversation in Website Content

There's a push-pull with website content that plenty of site owners or new companies face: You want to come across as professional and on brand, but you don't want the content to feel too structured or filled with jargon. If you go too far, you miss the opportunity to connect with readers through conversational content.

The web, online review sites, and social media have given the public a much greater say in the reputation of businesses. Unlike radio, print, or television, where the business owner defined the marketing message and pushed it out to millions of people, the internet gives people the opportunity to contribute their own dialogue in the form of reviews, social media, blogs, and more. Website development and maintenance should align with how businesses can open up conversations within their market. Leaning away from structured and solely professional language into a looser dialogue forges a deeper connection between you and your market.

Avoid Monologues in Your Website Copy

How do you know if content is conversational or not? It should feel like a dialogue between you and your reader. Of course, you won't actually be talking with them, but you want to imagine a conversation between your words on the screen and their mind as they read those words.

Thinking of your website content as a one-way street in which you craft a monologue based on your perception of the brand is a mistake.

For example, perhaps you assume it's the fact you've been in business for 25 years that keeps your customers coming back and referring you to friends. So a monologue-style text might be something like "Customers keep coming back because we've been here for 25 years." But customers themselves might use different wording. Perhaps you interview existing customers, who might reveal similar sentiments but in words such as the following:

- Quality and consistency
- Family business with a history of supporting the local community
- Track record of getting it done right the first time

If you only communicate to your consumers rather than getting and repurposing their feedback, you miss out on the unique opportunities available with interactive marketing.

What Is Conversational Content?

A conversation is a back and forth, in which your target audience sees your content and responds to it. Focusing on conversational content throughout your website copy can help you open an ongoing dialogue with your followers. Using conversational dialogue on your website helps improve your brand awareness and encourages engagement—a major benefit.

The primary foundation of conversational content is the ability to interrupt the other person at any point in time and to weave actual stories from your target market into your existing content. This is why you see fewer people talking only about their perception of their business and more sites incorporating social proof (actual customer feedback), testimonials, and snippets from reviews on their websites. Social proof helps back up the initial claims you make about your product or service.

Here's an example of making the same point in website copy with monologue-style and conversational content:

- *Monologue*: This company was founded on the principles of integrity and honesty, which drive us forward today as an insurance market leader.
- *Conversational*: I started this company because I felt like I couldn't get honest answers from my insurance agent. I don't want you to face the same hassle. That's why I put integrity and honesty first.

HEAR FROM THE EXPERTS
EXPERT: RUSHDA RAFEEK

Background: I have always wanted to be a writer. I remember holding my father's hand at a beach when I was little and listening to him say, "make sure you stay away from the pompous and delve more into the mundane. That's where the magic is—in the people, in their stories." This struck me and I decided to pick up the pen to create and tell stories people found fascinating. In doing so, I came to wear many hats of a word-slinger—copywriter, journalist, and editor. It's been three years since I experienced the full shebang of copywriting, the kind considered outside the box and strong enough to grip a wandering attention.

Understand that writing for the web is still writing for humans. The language you use should carry the weight of empathetic understanding about their needs, habits, and preferences at that exact moment. Rather than flabs of fanciful jargon, craft copy users may scan or skim smoothly. Think of online situations as rush hour. The honking noise and limited attention mean that a dent in your delivery or word choice can run the risk of goodbye forever. So then, would short sentences work? Most definitely. Your readers will stick around and read the whole page if it's precisely powerful. Believe me. It's something I learned the hard way. Also remember: Copy without proper sales psychology and research won't make a "killer" conversion. By offering insight-driven words, the art of true marketing will convey itself. Be clear about what to do next and let it resonate with what's really out there. Walk in their shoes if you have to.

Opening with conversational content also helps you learn a lot more about your target market. You can respond to questions quickly, capitalize on ideas that are gaining traction, and make faster decisions and pivots as needed.

Conversational writing anticipates a response or another form of engagement from a person reading it. This means conversational content is focused on your reader, not you. While it's a little different from a spoken conversation, the purpose is still to engage with readers and how they might respond in their heads.

Blogs, articles, and website copy will all strike a deeper chord with readers if you open a dialogue and continue a conversation in the reader's mind. As you write, try to lean into how you would speak to people instead of into formal writing. This can mean being more engaging and more casual with your language overall, but it does not mean you sacrifice a professional tone or perception.

By connecting with your readers through authentic conversational content, you break down the wall between your computer screens. Your client gets to know you and gets excited about the possibility of working with you.

Infusing the Art of Storytelling Into Your Website Copy

Storytelling is an art form as old as humans. Even though you might think of storytelling as a craft technique used by public speakers or fiction writers, every aspect of online marketing goes back to storytelling. People love good stories. You can have an excellent product, service, and team, but if you're not able to tell a good story about your company, you'll lose out on readership.

With storytelling in your website copy, you'll lean into the idea of beginning, middle, and end. As a company or person who helps solve the problems of others, your storytelling should connect with readers exactly where they are to serve them helpful and well-written material that answers their biggest questions.

What Makes a Good Story?

The essence of great storytelling in marketing today builds on the StoryBrand concept from Donald Miller's book of the same name.

Storytelling is often used to explain the craft techniques for writing fiction, but the truth is writing website copy should be no different. One thing that happens with far too much website content is that the owners of the website immediately launch into how the product or service has the potential to change the customer's life.

This comes off as very pitch-like, meaning the customer instinctively puts up a wall of resistance and disbelief about the claims being made. It is far better to begin the foundation of your website content with a good story to firmly place the reader in a position of trust. Then as the reader sees you as the thought leader and expert in the field, they can begin to imagine what you can do for them.

There's no doubt that your service or product offers a solution to a problem, but that problem must be identified and resolved within a story. That removes the reader's resistance to you selling to them. A story can encourage the reader's desire to get to the end result that your product or service provides. Storytelling is nothing new, but it is often overlooked on the web.

Chapter 1 Action Steps & Takeaways

- Determine the main reasons you need a website, especially the ones that speak best to your business goals.
- If you currently have a website, review it. Do you have conversational content on your website, or is your current content missing that element?
- Brainstorm: How can you infuse storytelling into your website?

Website Page Basics and How to Write Them

As a web browser yourself, you've probably noticed that while every site includes some common components, every site owner takes a slightly different approach to marketing their business online. For example, most websites will include an "about us" page and a way to contact them, but not all will include a blog or pricing information.

In this chapter, you'll learn about different kinds of website pages and content and how these can serve your overall marketing strategy.

How Does Design Impact My Site Pages?

Before we dive into talking about the words, a few quick notes on design. First, this is not a book on design principles, so we'll only touch on them briefly. For more information on website design, check out *Don't Make Me Think*, an excellent roadmap on how website visitors think and how to meet them where they are.

That said, words and design must work together for optimal site performance. Design and content should always work hand in hand, although they are two different skills, likely done by two different people. Your designer should have an awareness of the visual impression you're trying to make, and the writer brings a talent for words that complement the design.

When designers arrange your website, they often use templates that limit the volume of text for each page and section. This means a writer probably needs to target a specific word count for each part. If a block of text with an optimal maximum of 75 words, for example, has 150 words crammed in instead, the font size must be reduced. Otherwise, the text throws off the balance of the entire page.

Designers often provide a visual estimate of the text volume by putting in placeholder text, sometimes called Lorem ipsum. That way, you or the writer can see how much content might fit into that specific area.

User Experience for Website Design

For the best possible user experience, you want to limit the possibility that someone will get overwhelmed on your site. It's tempting to put out as much information as possible to show that you know what you're talking about, but this can backfire. A reader is likely to get confused about where to go next or feel overwhelmed by all the options. Remember, your website is your chance to build a relationship and open a conversation with your reader, so each page should be designed with that reader in mind.

A clean, simple interface on your home page with either a search bar or easy navigation will help someone who lands there find what they're looking for.

Although much of this book focuses on the craft of writing the website copy, don't overlook the other key element of developing your website: design. You can make it easy on yourself by outsourcing design to a team of professionals. Many drag-and-drop templates reflect good user experience principles, but outsourcing to a team of experts gives you confidence that they've done all the heavy lifting for you.

What Is the Ideal Website Structure?

Your website structure will dictate the total number of pages you need to write and the target length of each of those pages. Ideal sites will vary by industry and by the site owner's marketing plan. But a few basic guidelines apply to most site structures.

A well-organized website might look like a pyramid, starting with your home page, followed by sections or categories and then individual posts and pages. Your home page is the base for the entire website and you might list category or section pages beneath it. If you have a bigger site, you may also need subcategories.

When determining your core website structure, think about what your reader might be looking for on your page.

For a local restaurant, the reader might be looking for:

- Company history
- Menu
- Delivery or carryout options
- Hours of operation and locations

For a local service company, such as an oil change provider, the reader wants something different. They are probably seeking:

- Coupons
- Locations and hours
- Range of services and costs
- Online scheduling

For a product company, the reader might look for:

- Information about the owner
- The company's history, sourcing, or sustainability practices
- A shop
- Links to social media accounts

The experience for each of these readers is slightly different, although all these sites will include a home page and a contact page, at minimum. When you're drafting your own website structure, look at competitor sites. Notice what others are doing well and see if you can spot any industry trends in site layout.

CONTENT IS KING

Your home page is the welcome mat or navigation hub for every visitor to your website. This means your home page should include easy-to-use navigational pages to other important sections of the site. This shows Google that these pages are important and it helps your visitors navigate through the pages that are most important to them. But linking to too many pages from your home page will lead to clutter and confusion. Remember, your home page is a navigational tool to direct people to other locations. A web design team with a background in user experience can help you develop an appropriate site structure for your website.

Setting a Design Flow

Each website page and each section within that page should serve a purpose, leading the reader to a clear conclusion or action step. If the goal of your services page, for instance, is to get the reader to click into the smaller subservices pages, the design and the content on that page should drive readers toward that end.

If the purpose is to get readers to opt in to your email newsletter by signing up on a form at the bottom of the page, every item on that page should showcase your value and expertise so that readers want to learn more from you.

Where pages go wrong is in having no clear purpose or too many options for the reader. Because confused readers don't take action, you must very clearly break down what you want them to do.

Nontext Elements in Your Design

Websites use different kinds of design elements and visuals for different purposes. Let's look at a couple of examples.

Banners and Navigation

Navigational banners, usually at the top or sides of a website, break down content into smaller chunks. Some pages are informational, while others might be action-driven.

Here's an example of the menu options found on a skin-care company site. The company uses several tags at the top of the menu navigation:

Before & After, My Acne Story, Rewards, Shop, and Skin Quiz. I see two action-driven options: "Shop" and "Skin Quiz." The others, "Before & After," "My Acne Story," and "Rewards," are all informational in nature. The skin-care company is smart to use both words and visuals to tell their story. The "Before & After" page is an example of using social proof to sell products, but the additional step of adding personalization through the quiz and acne battle book also positions this company founder as an expert and thought leader in her field.

Imagery for Visual Product Sellers

When you run an ecommerce business, so much goes into getting the right visuals. But that doesn't mean the text doesn't matter. The product descriptions might include both general descriptions and hashtags to make it easier for the reader to find relevant information.

Visuals and design are important elements on every website, but even more so when you're selling physical products. A site like this will likely include pictures of the products you're selling. People want to see what they are getting and will use these visuals to make their final decision.

HEAR FROM THE EXPERTS
EXPERT: HALEY WALDEN

Background: I've been a copywriter for seven years. I write a variety of copy and marketing content styles, depending on the client's needs. My primary focuses are website copy, landing pages, and blog posts. I started out in digital marketing as a virtual assistant and quickly began putting my writing degree to use for clients who needed ghost-blogging. From there, I went on to form my own LLC.

It's helpful to have site wireframes on hand before you begin writing website copy. Knowing the general layout of the site BEFORE you write will help you know how much copy is needed, how it should be arranged, and how it will be presented on the website.

In this case, words help to describe the product. With a nonproduct company, the words do even more of the heavy lifting and you'll likely rely on fewer photos.

Design or Write First?

There are mixed opinions on whether you should wait to write your website copy until you have the design finished or vice versa. For those who are new to website writing, it can be a lot easier to get the design or template in place first so you can visualize how much text you're looking for on each page.

Website Content Types: A Basic Overview

While your website will always contain some unique elements from your industry, most websites include similar types of content. Knowing which ones are most relevant for your needs will help you create a roadmap for your site. Each website page should function well on its own and as part of the site as a whole.

Whether you're planning to write your own content or to hire a freelance writer to do it, defining the pages you'll need is the first step to getting the project done. What follows are brief introductions to the kinds of content you're most likely to need. In this chapter, you'll learn about individual website pages you'll need to launch, and in Part II of this book, beginning with Chapter 7, you'll learn about supplemental materials you might use as part of your content marketing strategy.

In addition to the content you publish on your site, you'll also develop other pieces of content as part of your marketing plan. Modern businesses use content marketing to drive traffic to their company website and platforms, but the entire ecosystem of content creation requires thinking about each of these components.

Other pieces of content marketing include:

- Press releases
- Infographics
- Images with text overlay for social media
- Social media text-based posts

Home Page

General length: flexible

In terms of content, your home page is very flexible. You can include lots of graphics, photos, and videos if that will help your ideal audience to interact with you and your site more effectively. For the purposes of search engines, however, it's a good idea to have some base text on your home page that explains who you are, what you do, and who you do that for, so a person finding your site can easily and quickly decide if they're in the right place.

Your home page is the place where you have the best chance to make an impression with your brand. You'll combine the visual aspects of your site design with text to share your company's story and positioning.

Review and update your home page twice a year. Many companies use rotating versions of their home page, so different visitors receive different versions of the site. Doing this can provide you with helpful information and data about which messages resonate best with your audience, which allows you to eliminate underperformers. Sometimes varying home pages can provide a better user experience overall, when someone is navigating back to the home page again and again. Having a few different versions of your home page that are continually updated and evaluated can have big impacts.

And don't overlook small opportunities to increase your conversions to email newsletter sign-ups. You can make changes as small as swapping out one word in that sign-up text or tweaking the background color of the button. Internet marketing and content marketing are all about making and then testing hypotheses. Those results will drive any changes or updates to your material. Even if you've invested a great deal of time and money in a well-written home page, remember to review it regularly. If several months or a year has passed since it was last updated, it might be time to take a look at whether it still resonates with your target audience.

For well over a year, I used copy on my own business website talking about helping freelancers start their business. While a lot of people visiting my site were beginning their freelance content writing business, others were more established and had a whole different set of needs and concerns.

CONTENT IS KING

I installed different versions of my home page with a question asking readers where they were on their freelance journey. That way, I could align the story line with their personal needs. Beginners were directed to a suite of beginner resources and a page talking about my own experience launching my freelance business and helping others do the same. I directed advanced clients to resources aimed at the needs of a scaling entrepreneur.

About Page

General length: 300 to 600 words

One of the best places to showcase personality on your website is your about page. This is where you fuse your industry background with some of your personal interests, hobbies, and approaches to business. If you only have a few members on your team, your about page might include a biography for each of them, or it could speak from a big-picture perspective about why you started the company and the missions and values that drive your business today.

Allow your company's individualism to shine through in an about page. If you take a nontraditional approach to doing business or if you've racked up numerous industry awards, the about page is the place to list this.

Here are some questions to help you jump-start the process of drafting an about page:

- Whom do we help? What is their primary crisis or need when they call or hire us?
- Why did our founders start this business? How has the company evolved since then?
- How long have individual team members or the entire company been in business?
- What makes our company different from our competitors?
- Have we received any special distinctions or honors, such as specific awards, industry recognition from organizations or conferences, or exceptional customer feedback and testimonials?
- Are there any unique aspects of our company culture or values that we want our customers to know?

Services Pages: For Service-Based Companies Only

General length: 500+ words

Services pages are where you get to provide more information about the core services your business offers. Properly leveraging services pages accomplishes a few goals. First, these pages highlight your knowledge of individual services, confirming that you can help with your readers' specific concerns. Secondly, services pages are a great place to provide additional information and education about the reader's primary problem or pain point. A CPA business, for example, might have services pages that look like this:

- General bookkeeping and account reconciliation
- Annual tax filing
- LLC and S corp setup help
- IRS problems and back taxes

Readers can use these pages to find the material most relevant for their immediate needs. On these longer pages, they can learn about both the issue in question and your individual approach to helping customers with this problem. For the IRS problems and back taxes services page, for example, the CPA might explain their typical intake process, in addition to giving examples of cases in which they've helped people with IRS issues. This combination of industry-specific knowledge that meets and builds the consumer's trust can pave the path for future business.

A motivational speaker's services pages will look different. These might include:

- Keynotes
- Corporate workshops
- Speaker coaching
- National conference sessions

To get started with services pages, take a look at your competitors and think about the key services you want to promote within your business. The services pages allow your readers to get more information on a very specific offering, so choose carefully what you select.

Not everyone needs services pages. As the name suggests, they are most relevant for professionals running a service business.

Here are some questions to help you think about what services pages to include on your website:

- What are the major benefits you can offer clients and customers at this point in time?
- What are the different ways that people can work with you or your company?
- Are you trying to target certain keywords? For example, keywords such as "beach wedding planner in Miami" might deserve their own services page called "Miami Beach Weddings."

FAQs

General length: 600 to 1,000 words

A frequently asked questions (FAQ) page accomplishes a few goals for your company. First of all, it limits the time your customer service or reception employees spend answering the same questions. An FAQ page can also help boost your search engine rankings because it will include many of the same keywords that your customers would. This page can help tell Google what your website is all about.

A typical FAQ page will include at least five questions with answers. You can craft the text from questions you've often been asked or concerns you think most potential customers might have.

For a service-based business, an FAQ page might explain how the service works, whether refunds are offered, and how much lead time is typically required to schedule the service.

An FAQ section might be located on your home page or on its own page. This is the place to address the most common business questions you receive.

Blogs

General length: 300+ words

A blog is one of the most important components of any website marketing strategy. While "About Us" or your home page are likely to remain the same over time, your blog is your company's chance to send consistent signals to search engines about your primary keywords and focus topics

HEAR FROM THE EXPERTS
EXPERT: EMILY DALAMANGAS

Background: I have been a copywriter with my own business for two years. Prior to that, I worked for 20 years in marketing for media companies including Reuters, Condé Nast, and Hearst.

If you have random bits of information that do not belong in your other website sections, then create an FAQ section and add those details there. An FAQ section is effective for showing your potential clients that you are knowledgeable in your area of expertise and are covering questions they may not even think to ask.

while also engaging your customers on a regular basis. Many companies write at least two to four new blog posts per month.

Blog length can vary. Google tends to reward the quality of content rather than the quantity, but no blog should be less than 300 words, especially if you're only posting once per week. If you plan to post daily with similar topics and keywords, 300 to 400 words should be sufficient. If you only post once per week, make it count and aim for at least 800 words.

Blogs can expand on frequently asked questions, highlight industry news, and address topics and how-to guides for your ideal readers. Because blogs are updated more frequently than static pages, blog topics should line up with the season whenever possible.

The blogging chapters in this book, Chapters 9 and 10, go into more detail about blogging strategy, including selecting keywords, choosing topics, and structuring posts.

Landing Pages

General length: 500+ words

Depending on whom you talk to, a landing page could include a short piece of copy or it could include a lot of detail about a particular topic. The traditional definition of a landing page refers to a page that offers a lead magnet to your client in exchange for their email address. A lead magnet is any piece of free material directly related to the customer's biggest pain point at that moment.

On a landing page, you'll explore a major topic in a way that inspires your customer to contact you. Imagine a personal injury lawyer who mostly represents victims of traumatic brain injury (TBI). That attorney might have a long-form landing page dedicated to car accidents and TBI. This page could include informational details about studies on the connection between car accidents and TBI, how TBI is diagnosed, the possible costs and recovery period for a TBI victim, and the extent to which negligence plays a role in a TBI victim getting financial support for recovery. At the conclusion of this long page, the attorney might ask the reader to fill out a contact form or schedule a free consultation.

In this way, a long-form landing page does more than educate your reader about a topic of importance. It also positions you as someone with expert-level knowledge within your industry. Consumers are much more likely to reach out when you've built the foundation of a trusting relationship by providing reliable, relevant information about the subjects they are most interested in when they land on your page.

Sales Pages

General length: 1,000 to 2500 words

The purpose of a sales page is very simple: to prompt someone to buy something. There's both an art and a science to sales pages and they can be some of the most difficult to write. Whether you're selling an online course, coaching, or other services, a sales page takes the reader on a psychological journey starting with their pain point and ending with the proposed solution (your service or product).

Because sales pages make the biggest ask of readers in pulling out their credit or debit card to purchase something, they can be some of the most complex to write. Some sales pages can take even an experienced writer up to 10 hours because of the many rounds of revision and fine-tuning. However, the magic of a well-written sales page can be music to your ears when it works, because this is one avenue of your website that directly brings in income.

Sales pages alone are often not enough to build the know, like, and trust relationship for a first-time buyer. It's far more likely that a follower opts in to your lead magnet, follows your newsletter or blog for some time, and then later decides to make a direct purchase from you.

Plenty of businesses won't make direct use of sales pages. If your marketing structure converts more effectively with in-person meetings, phone consultations, or live events, you might not need sales pages for your site.

If sales pages, landing pages, and lead magnets are relevant for your business, you can learn more about them in Chapter 11.

Product Pages

General length: Flexible

If you sell mostly digital or physical products, you might use product pages in lieu of services pages. Usually, the copy on these pages is relatively brief, unless you're explaining a complex product or process. You can certainly go into more detail when it makes sense to do so, but try to keep things short and sweet with products. Your reader will likely look at other material about the product like reviews or videos, too.

Here's an example for a product page:

The Alphalyzer reading tool for kids is the number one choice for parents looking to help their children learn to read quickly. With over 5,000 reviews from happy parents, we know your child will love the process of picking up books and learning new words each day.

The Alphalyzer includes features like:

- Friendly, natural voices that reward your child as they reach reading milestones
- Colorful, easy-to-use display that works for parents and kids
- No ongoing software fees or subscriptions
- Barcode scanner for any book to read it aloud and allow your child to follow along

Other Important Pages

In addition to these pages, don't forget about basics such as:

- ⚡ Your company's terms
- ⚡ Your company's privacy policy

These are especially important in modern times, when you need to provide details about how you collect and use customers' data. Plenty of companies overlook these. You can purchase boilerplate privacy policies and similar templates, but make sure you read through what you're getting. You might be better off with a lawyer who can customize this material for you. Your privacy policy and terms tell people what you do with website visitor data, and these pieces are usually linked in the footer of your website.

Creating Your Website Roadmap

A website roadmap provides not only a pathway for the content creator or freelance writer, but it also increases the chances of success with your website designer. Your designer will use your roadmap to build a site that your readers can easily navigate. Finalizing your primary website topics upfront makes it easier for the designer to decide how to lay things out visually.

To get there, start by breaking down your ideas into the pages that are most necessary for your readers. Create a brain dump list of possibilities and come back to it a few times to trim things down. Simple is always best, and remember that you'll be able to link to other pages on the site as you go.

Now that you know the types of pages you'll need for most websites, let's look at an example of one service professional's roadmap. A life coach is likely to use both services pages and sales pages on their site. Here's how they might sketch out their roadmap.

Life Coach Website Example Roadmap

1. Home page
2. About us page
3. Services page: Group/mastermind coaching

4. Services page: Three-month one-on-one coaching
5. Services page: Strategy sessions
6. Blog-style page: Podcast
7. Blog-style page: Text blog
8. FAQs
9. Contact me
10. Short-form landing page: Lead magnet (Three Ways to Get Your Life Back on Track after a Transition)
11. Sales page: Mastering Your Life as an Empty Nester Course

Putting together a content roadmap makes it easy for everyone involved in the content creation process to see what needs to be completed and what aspects, if any, require regular updating. As the above example shows, the website might need two separate pages for new content—in this case, podcast episodes and new blogs. The other pages will likely keep the same content all the time or require minimal updates.

Chapter 2 Action Steps & Takeaways

- Recognize the ways that good design supports great content.
- Brainstorm a possible website structure: What pages do you think your site needs to launch?
- Start thinking about which elements of your brand you might include on your home page, about page, services pages, and other pages.

Defining Your Unique Value Proposition

You can't make an impact through search engines or connect with your target customer unless you have a way to explain what makes you stand out. Standing out is important for businesses of all sizes, whether you're a local company or a worldwide brand.

Understanding a company's unique value proposition (UVP), or what makes you distinct from your competitors, is the gateway to crafting all content strategy and copy. This UVP should be infused throughout your copy and your site.

The process of finding your UVP is also part of finding your voice. Your main goal is to make it clear to your ideal customer when they land on your website that you are the right business for them. You want your audience to read your copy and say "Wow, it feels like they are talking directly to me. This company understands me."

In this chapter, you will learn about your target audience and how to connect authentically with them.

What's in a UVP?

A UVP is your secret sauce. It's what makes you distinct from all the other competitors on the market. If your product is so innovative that you don't have many direct competitors, your UVP might be that you've evolved a product or industry to meet the needs of a target population.

Your UVP is *not* a slogan, a tag line, or your mission statement. Your UVP is all about the benefits you offer to customers.

You cannot and should not copy the tag line, motto, or guarantee of another competitor. Because here's what's so key about the unique value proposition: for it to be unique, it must apply to only your business.

Here are some examples of unique value propositions. This list is not all-inclusive, but it's a good place to get started:

- Speed
- Delivery schedule
- Quality of product
- Years of experience
- Highly rated or reviewed
- Customer retention rate
- Relatability or humanity
- Giving back to your local community
- Company culture

Or you may combine a few ideas for your UVP.

Need more inspiration? Let's take a look at some existing companies who have pinned down a solid UVP.

For Eversign, a digital signature platform, the UVP is "Legally binding electronic signatures at work, at home, or on the go." A UVP might be the same as your tag line.

For the massive online open course platform Coursera, the UVP is "Learn without limits."

For Unbounce, a landing page company, the UVP is "Build, publish, and A/B test landing pages without IT."

Every one of these UVPs is customer-centric and delivers a clear explanation of what the company does. They're concise and attention-getting, too.

What's Your UVP: Whom Do You Serve?

The real power in website copy is connecting your UVP with your customer's primary needs and concerns. Both pieces are necessary to forge a connection with your audience.

If there's a cardinal branding sin companies make, it's saying "but everyone is my customer." Yes, theoretically, if you sell trash bags or forks or something ubiquitous, your target customer *could* be anyone.

But by focusing on everyone, you're focusing on no one. Think about Walmart. In theory, the store has a broad customer base that could include anyone. But that's not the ideal Walmart shopper. Walmart's target customer is someone who wants great prices and wants to get all their shopping done in one store, knowing they're probably getting the lowest prices on 90 percent of those purchases.

Walmart is not trying to appeal to the same luxury buyer that watch brand Rolex is targeting. Both companies know that their target customer is not everyone, and they go out of their way in their marketing to prove it.

If your target audience up until now has been everyone, it's time to hit the drawing board again. Narrow down your market again and again until you can speak clearly to whom you're trying to reach. If you come up with three or four different people, those are your buyer personas. You'll address each of those buyer personas in your website copy based on how important they are to your overall marketing strategy.

One of the most important things you can do, not just to make a first impression but also to keep the right kinds of clients and followers on your site, is to highlight your UVP.

While a small section of your customers might be looking for the first company they find, that's increasingly rare. People have a lot of choices, and with no way to differentiate between your business and everyone else, they will default to things like price or average review. Neither of these serves your business in the best way possible.

Selecting a UVP can be overwhelming for new companies, but start by coming up with three words that describe your brand. Choosing between two and five ways to stand out is important.

How to Find Your UVP

Your best source of your UVP is current customers, if you have them. However, you can still find a great UVP if your company is new.

When I first started my freelance copywriting business, I thought for sure that my UVP would be my years of experience in the legal field. I relied heavily on that messaging to get my first 50 or so clients. But then I spotted a trend: all my clients pointed out one or two things over and over. They'd either say "you're so easy to work with" or "your work doesn't need many revisions at all" or both of those statements.

As a writer, those seemed like obvious things. Wouldn't any business-person be easy to work with? How could they stay in business if they were difficult? And wouldn't those same writers strive to turn in work that was as polished as possible? But it really didn't matter what I thought. What was important was that my clients were telling me my new UVP. I was an experienced legal copywriter who was easy to work with, who got the job done right the first time around. I instantly pivoted my messaging to match. That had a twofold effect. Those existing happy clients referred me to more and more clients who had similar things to say about me, and I also developed more long-term relationships with my current clients (including a monthly retainer client I've worked with for nine years as of the writing of this book).

Don't try to invent your UVP if you can help it. Lean into what you're already naturally good at, and excel at delivering that message to customers or clients who connect with those attributes.

If you can only compete with everyone else on price, that quickly becomes a race to the bottom. And for some clients or customers, prices that get lower and lower just raise suspicion about quality.

If your reader defaults to average review, that might work out in your favor. But ultimately, the best you can do to control reviews is ask happy customers to leave one. Setting up messaging with your UVP is within your control and might even be a way to back up the social proof you have from reviews.

To be clear, I'm not saying your company can overcome really bad reviews or questionable pricing by having good messaging. Good messaging will always help, but it's part of a bigger strategy to put your best foot forward. If you're an existing business with bad reviews or other issues, address those at the same time that you work on your website content strategy.

Figure 3.1 on page 36 shows some potential brand values you can review to see what jumps out at you. Remember, choose no more than five. You cannot be everything to everyone.

Find Your Ideal Customers . . . and What They Need

If you can, start joining places where your ideal customers spend time. If you're a product business, read the reviews of competitors' products on major retail sites to make notes of what people didn't like. This can also help confirm your product marketing strategy and give you clues about whether you're on the right track. Mining the places where your audience spends time has a twofold purpose here. You can determine your own UVP, but it also helps you understand the problems your audience has and the language they use to describe them. Make a list of terms and concepts that pop up again and again.

Here's an example:

Let's say you're a productivity coach looking to create website copy that helps you stand out from the many blogs, resources, and other coaches in this space. You might dig through places like AnswerThePublic and Quora to see the most common questions people bring up. If your audience is solopreneurs, you might join social media groups full of entrepreneurs to see what kinds of questions they ask. Screenshot or save those posts if you spot them in the moment but need to review them later. You might learn that the idea of digital overwhelm pops up again and again. People are overloaded by their email inboxes and looking for ways to cut clutter. Perhaps you find that people use phrases like "it's too much" and "I'm buried in emails" to describe the challenges they face.

Accountable	Knowledgeable
Altruistic	Loyal
Ambitious	Magnetic
Analytical	Methodical
Brave	Modern
Caring	Organized
Clean	Outgoing
Clever	Outspoken
Collaborative	Natural
Comforting	Passionate
Committed	Persistent
Conservative	Polished
Considerate	Practical
Contemporary	Progressive
Courageous	Purposeful
Daring	Receptive
Decisive	Reliable
Determined	Resilient
Diplomatic	Responsible
Disruptive	Robust
Driven	Sensible
Dynamic	Serious
Educated	Sharp
Encouraging	Structured
Entertaining	Stunning
Exclusive	Successful
Expert	Systematic
Focused	Timeless
Fresh	Traditional
Friendly	Trustworthy
Honest	Unconventional
Imaginative	Understanding
Ingenious	Unprecedented
Inquisitive	Vivacious
Insightful	Zealous

FIGURE 3.1: **Potential Brand Values**

From here, you can create a UVP around how your productivity resources and coaching can get them back on track quickly. In this case, you've used a customer pain point to craft what makes you different while also appealing to them directly by using their own words.

Pro tip: A great way to amplify the research you find online is to talk to actual people. There is no good replacement for speaking to people to learn about their challenges. If you can get 20 or more people in your target market to talk to you, ask them questions and record the conversation to discover their biggest challenges. One common mistake that plenty of interviewers make here is to start with leading questions, such as "I'm building my website copy around my new project management software. Do you think this sounds like a good idea as a product?" People, especially those who know you, will be eager to validate your idea or support you, so they won't tell you the truth.

Here's a better opening question: "I'm working on a new project to learn how business owners organize their projects. Can you tell me the biggest challenges you face when it comes to organization?"

The primary distinction here is that the second question lets the customer lead. You're not feeding them any advance information. Instead, you're getting valuable information about what they truly find to be their biggest challenge. A great resource for making sure you're asking the right questions is a book called *The Mom Test*, by Rob Fitzpatrick.

How to Find Your UVP If You're Already in Business

If you already have customers, they are the most solid source of a UVP. They'll save you thousands of dollars or lots of time in market research because they can tell you either why they keep coming back to you, why someone else wasn't a fit, or both. You'll find lots of clues in the feedback you receive, either directly or indirectly, so start by mining that if you have it.

If you don't have written feedback or reviews yet, ask your customers questions like:

- How would you describe us to a friend?
- What three words come to mind when thinking about our company and our offerings?

- What was the best part about working with us?
- What made you decide to go with us rather than someone else?

Surveying or interviewing your current customers is a great supplement to reading existing reviews of your business. If you already have great clients or customers, focusing on what brought them to you only helps attract other like-minded people.

How to Find Your UVP If You're New

Know that if you're new, your UVP might evolve over time and that's OK. You still need an angle to start with, especially if you'll primarily share it in places that can be updated quickly, like your website.

You started your company for a reason, and some of that reason might be a lack of options in the marketplace. Your product or service might also be your passion. Those are excellent starting points for crafting a UVP.

To find your UVP, you need to do a deep dive on all your current competition. If you've ever been through a founder's or tech accelerator, you'll spend days or weeks analyzing the existing competition. Even if the company you're starting is not truly comparable to any of the current solutions out there, these accelerator mentors will tell you that your idea is not new. In one such session, a mentor of mine told me that a competitor for my idea for a list-creating software was a pen and paper! And he was right.

So look for all the other ways people are currently solving the problem you're addressing. Look at how they've defined their UVP. One of the easier ways to tap into your own UVP is to evaluate the competition, so you can concisely and directly compare your offering to theirs.

Your distinguishing factors might be things like:

- A better customer experience
- A service or product that is easier to use
- A more streamlined process
- Faster shipping
- Combining multistep processes or software programs into one hub
- Removing the hassle associated with something traditionally difficult

Here are some examples of really clear UVPs that make it all about the customer:

- *TurboTax* makes it easy for people to file and submit their taxes digitally without an accountant. It's a good fit for people with simple tax situations who don't want to go through the hassle of finding a CPA or waiting weeks for a refund. Users are guided through a step-by-step process, get reminders from the software when they haven't submitted yet, and can easily check the status of their refund check and return submission online.
- *No BS Active*, a video-content exercise app, targets people who want to work out from home with fun trainers. With their subscription service, users get a new workout video five days a week from two trainers. One trainer, a popular reality TV star known for her personality, offers modifications for people with injuries or other special needs. This service is geared toward people who can't or don't want to go to the gym, might be nervous about exercising, and who want to connect with a fun-loving reality star for daily exercise.
- *BrainPOP*, an educational tool, provides short lessons with a cartoon man and robot for all kinds of school subjects. It's a great way for teachers to introduce something complex in an attention-grabbing and understandable way.

Each of these examples has taken a traditional problem, such as finding and working with an accountant or how to get in a workout when you don't want to go to the gym and need modifications, and made solving that problem their UVP.

Creating a UVP for a Solo Business Owner

The resources and strength of your team are compelling benefits of working with bigger companies, but solopreneurs can infuse more of their personality throughout their UVP than bigger companies can. Emphasizing what you love and what is most important to you can dramatically increase the chances that someone not only connects with your copy but also with you as a person. In many solopreneur businesses, in fact, your customer is purchasing *you* rather than the service or the product you provide.

They believe in what you do and who you are, and the more you can sprinkle this throughout your website content and copy, the more successful you'll be. To figure out your solopreneur UVP, start by creating a list of what you love. This could include the following:

- TV shows or books you're obsessed with and turn to again and again
- Activities that make up the majority of your free time and you wish you could do more of
- Music genres or hobbies that make you feel alive
- Celebrities or experts you follow and respect

From there you can brainstorm additional ideas, such as synonyms related to your core personality. Check out a thesaurus and look for words that describe who you are and what you do. For example, imagine that some of your past clients have commented on how energetic you are and see this as an advantage of working with you. They are buying into your energy. To brainstorm beyond that word and think about how you can work this idea into your UVP, search for synonyms along the lines of *zestful, animated, vibrant, bouncy, lively, sparkling,* or *perky.*

What If We Don't Have a UVP?

I've worked with hundreds of law firms on their website copy, and most of the time they discover their UVP during a conversation with me. Sometimes it seems so subtle to them that they don't even see how a trait could be used to help them stand out. For example, one firm I worked with was adamant that all any legal client cared about was experience and professionalism. I told the firm's owner that I believed those were the core of any law firm but that plenty of clients were looking far beyond that.

Remember that confused customers don't buy. So if 50 personal injury law firms in a car accident victim's regional area all appear relatively capable and professional, that potential client will just call the first one listed alphabetically or the one with the best reviews.

As the law firm owner and I continued our conversation, he dropped gold nuggets about their UVP left and right without realizing it.

"We don't ever pass off cases to an associate. The lawyer who brings the case in handles everything, including all communication."

"We settle about 60 percent of our cases because we're able to get a fair result that makes our clients happy and it saves on further litigation time and expense."

These were both great things to work into the UVP.

The Right UVP Attracts the Right Customers

Pinning down your UVP is really important because it helps you determine whether you're bringing in the right followers. But there's another reason to invest in developing and refining your UVP: The right UVP attracts the right people and repels the wrong ones.

Consider the law firm example mentioned above. As we wove the story line of personalized attention from the same attorney you felt confident in hiring, we struck a chord with the potential clients who were worried about working with a "big firm" and never knowing where their case was. But potential clients who wanted someone to doggedly take their case to trial, even if it took years, would also know this firm was *not* the best fit for them.

How to Define and Use Audience Personas

An audience, user, or buyer persona is like an ideal client avatar. You're diving deeper into who your target customer is, their primary problems, what they're looking for in a solution, and any demographic information about them as a whole.

It's very possible that you have more than one buyer persona. On your general website, you'll want to appeal to either the biggest group of your customers or equally among different personas who are all your target customers. For other content, such as blogs or social media, you might use a specific buyer persona for each piece of content.

Imagine that you're a pet-sitter starting your business in a new location. When creating your website content, you've got at least two buyer personas to consider:

> *Vacation Victoria*, who only needs help when she's out for a week or longer. She's a single professional who wishes she could take her dog with her on vacation, but she wants to know that he's having a

good time and is well taken care of when she steps out. She wants someone she can trust in her house, too. She might only contact you a few times a year, but when she does, it's for a big stay.

- *Working William*, who is looking for a dog walker/pet-sitter who can check on his animals once a day while he's at his job for a 12-hour shift. William is looking for someone reliable who will show up consistently, as well as someone who can form a long-term bond with his dog.

Both of these buyer personas could be potential customers of the service or product, but they have slightly different needs. In your website copy, you might cover both of their concerns individually, or you could speak generally to what they have in common. Either approach can be successful.

HEAR FROM THE EXPERTS
EXPERT: RACHEL C. BOLLER

Background: I started copywriting three years ago, but I've been writing for longer. I've written everything from website copy, email marketing newsletters, client recipes (I'm a former pastry chef, so this is related to my niche), and social media copy to product packaging and label copy.

Before engaging a web developer or building a site yourself (and definitely before writing out copy), take some time to think about your target audience and what you want them to *do* when they hit your page. Flesh out your ideal customer as clearly as possible, and think through the steps they need to take to work with you. Do they need to book a discovery call? Or email you? Or should they fill out a short contact form? Work backward from that action and make it as easy as possible for your ideal customer to take that next action with clear language and call to action buttons. Don't make them hunt for an obscure page or button that has too clever a name. Another tip: Define your UVP before writing anything else. Without having to scroll too much, your user should understand who you are, what you do, who you do it for, and why you're so good at it.

Use Survey Data to Assess Your Audience Persona

If you're building a website but are unsure of your audience/buyer persona, you can learn a lot about them through survey research. You can hire survey companies to help you get direct feedback from your target market and learn more about what is most important to your audience. With Google surveys and companies like SurveyMonkey, you pay a specific amount of money for each survey result, which varies from a dime to several dollars per survey completion.

One of the best things about not having an existing audience persona is that you have the chance to be creative. You can also tap directly into the market in real time and build the data you gleaned right back into your marketing plan.

If you have the opportunity to use open-ended questions in your survey, you can learn the exact words and phrases that your audience uses. Make sure your survey questions directly request the feedback and information that you need to build this brand persona. You can then use the responses to better understand these demographics and develop an audience content persona. If you have access to your target audience outside of surveys, such as people in your direct network, consider setting up customer informational interviews. These can last 20 to 30 minutes and tell you more about this person's primary concerns.

What Questions Should I Ask in My Survey or Interview?

Start with basic demographic information about your audience member, such as name, gender, age, location, where they work, job title, industry, and the biggest challenges they face. You might also add questions that drill down further into your specific business type. This kind of data can help you understand where most of your audience members share commonalities.

How to Learn More about Your Target Audience Through Social Media

Yes, your audience is interested in solving the specific problem you're presenting, but they are also dynamic people with other interests and concerns. Some of those interests and concerns will be shared by a good portion of your audience. For example, imagine that your ideal audience member is interested in home renovation. You could make a reasonable assumption that they like HGTV or visit BobVila.com. That same person might also be interested in flea markets or other DIY projects. Adding these kinds of guesses is how you build out a more comprehensive version of your target audience member.

Something awesome about living in the modern era is that someone has probably already done the work of collecting information about your target audience. (We can save the privacy debates for another day.) Hello, big data!

Head on over to Facebook and type into the search bar "interests liked by people who like _____." Fill in the blank with the name of a competitor or another interest of your ideal audience member.

You'll get a list of information about your target audience members and other things they like. You can use this material to provide context and also to highlight those other details throughout your copy.

Let's imagine you're a closet organization company who found that your audience is also interested in home renovations and DIY projects. But your premise is that they don't know how to get started with organizing a functional closet. You might use that in a line of copy, such as "Keep your weekends for watching *Property Brothers* and let us do the heavy lifting. You'll head into each week with the knowledge that your closet is fully organized and ready for action during the busy work and school days."

That kind of copy is what makes your audience feel like you're talking directly to them. It works because you've done your research to confirm what they like and their levels of interest.

How to Use Facebook Audience Insights to Learn about Your Buyer Persona

Facebook audience insights are tools used by online marketers to learn more about the vast data treasure trove that is Facebook. You can look at people who are connected to your personal page or all of Facebook. There is very little reason to look at the information connected to your page audience, especially if you have an audience segment of fewer than 1,000 people. Start by looking more broadly at all of Facebook and then adding differentiating factors to help narrow this down.

Navigate to Facebook.com\ads\audience-insights. In the interests section, type in your industry or other terminology people would use to describe your industry. Then narrow down by demographic information. You can gather a great deal of valuable data in this process. Don't forget to look at the lifestyle section of the Facebook audience insights to identify goals and challenges of your potential target readers.

Your copy should always be based on your UVP and what is most helpful to your target customers. In this chapter, you learned how to evaluate and describe your audience so you can craft copy about what you can offer to them. In the next chapter, you'll learn how to incorporate these elements into your content marketing strategy.

Chapter 3 Action Steps & Takeaways

- Determine whom you serve and how that influences your company's unique value proposition.
- Think about brand value adjectives that can set you apart from your competition and clearly convey what's most important about your brand.
- Survey your current or prospective customers to learn more about what's most important to them (or use social media).
- Determine your audience personas for your business.
- Define your unique value proposition.

Writing Copy: Best Practices and Brand Guidelines

Now that you know what your brand stands for and what you'd like to communicate to your target audience, it's time to think about how that information forms the basis of good copy. You don't want to end up with "word salad" (a bunch of words thrown up there, but without much strategy behind them). That is not useful to you or, more importantly, to your ideal client or customer.

General Copywriting Principles for Your Entire Website

Remember to make your website engaging to your reader. That reader is ultimately the person who connects with your product or service. In this section, you'll learn the most important tips to keep in mind as you craft your content.

The more you can continue to connect with your target reader and deploy the same copywriting principles throughout your site, the more consistent your marketing messages will be, too. Review these principles every time you prepare to write new content or update existing content to keep them top of mind.

Tip 1: Educate Rather Than Sell

You might assume that the primary function of your website and its content is to sell your services or products. An underlying element of sales does run through a comprehensive website. But the primary focus of all content you create should be to educate and support your target customer.

When you tell people helpful information that answers a question or fear they have, you build a trusting relationship as a person or company of authority. Although ultimately your goal is to convert that reader into a paying client or customer, start by giving first. Most readers can tell when they are being sold to and may resist trusting your expertise if you lean into a hard sell too early.

Tip 2: Be Relatable in Your Content

One of the most important components of engaging content is relatability. Even if you are a professional services provider whose education or expertise is important to telling your story, you still need to be relatable and accessible to your audience. The helpful tone combined with the engaging capability of your content will not only get readers to the page but encourage them to stay there. This also increases the chances they will share your content with others, leave comments, or engage in other activity directly with your content.

To be more relatable, it's OK to talk about mistakes and to demystify complex processes. Never assume that your reader is stupid or doesn't have some context of the topic, so you want to strike a balance between giving helpful information without being too complex or high-level for your content to resonate with the reader.

Tip 3: Don't Use All Caps

This one is relatively simple, but it's powerful. Be aware of not just the words you write but also the way that those words show up. This gets a little bit into design, as well, since the formatting and font selections you make can have a big impact.

Other format options are available to make your point. I love using italics to indicate that I'm being sarcastic or that I would lean into a particular word if I were speaking it. All caps is visually distracting and difficult to read, so use formatting tools such as bold, underline, or italics instead.

Tip 4: Check Your Content for Duplication

Whether intentionally or by accident, you might wind up with copy on your website that matches another person's page. This is known as duplicate content and it's not only plagiarism; it can be harmful to your efforts to rank your website for chosen keywords.

Duplicate content can be entire chunks of text or simply longer phrases. More often than not, you won't have duplicate content if you wrote your website copy yourself. This comes up more frequently when a company outsources their content to a writer, doesn't check the work for duplication, and then later finds out it was stolen.

Content writers should do proper research to ensure their work is original. Use tools such as Copyscape.com to pay pennies per 500 words searched. This will give you peace of mind that your content has not been stolen. Content should always be 100 percent original.

Tip 5: Make Sure Each Website Page Has a Clear Beginning, Middle, and End

The material in each section of your website pages should be balanced between the introduction and conclusion. For most pages, the middle is where you'll have the bulk of the content. In this case, do a final review of every page you create to make sure it's clear from a reader's perspective what the beginning, middle, and end of every single page is.

As you review pages, pay attention to the journey you take your reader through. Does the end of the piece deliver on the promise made in the title?

If you told someone they'd learn a six-step process, did you cover all six steps clearly? Did you include images or other explanations to help make that process easier to digest? These are just a few examples of how you can bring a reader through a journey in each individual page so that the premise of the page delivers on the promise of the page.

Tip 6: Always Check for Grammar and Spelling Errors

This one should be obvious, but it's also hard to fit into your strategy if you don't have the right people or tools to make it happen. Errors can and do slip by, and they can cost you some credibility points.

Sidenote: It really is not the end of the world if you have a typo on your website, but it's best to avoid them if possible. Especially if you're in a detail-oriented industry or if writing ability is part of your business (authors, social media managers, freelance writers, marketing strategists), you can expect to receive emails from people who spot typos on your website.

Thankfully, simple routes exist to solving this problem. The first is to hire a proofreader. If you're not producing ongoing content, your proofreader can help you for a one-time project. You can deliver all your completed website content pages to them after you've written the drafts, and then after the proofread, you'll publish all those pages together. Frankly, whether you write your content yourself or hire a freelance writer to craft it for you, consider proofreading your final step of the publishing process.

Having a completely different person proofread your material prevents any mistakes made from tunnel vision, which can happen when you stare at the same content for a long time or when you've been stuck on how to write a certain page.

You can also use tools such as Grammarly or the Hemingway App to spot-check your work if you're not working with a proofreader. They both provide helpful tips to make sure your finished work is as polished as possible.

Tip 7: Edit for Conciseness, and Then Edit Again

Resist the temptation to assume that having more words is better. All too often, websites are too long, meaning many readers will not scroll past the part of the page that first appears on their screen. Factor in the impact of mobile viewing and this becomes even more important. Get the words on the page for an initial first draft, and then go back later with fresh eyes to cut and then cut again. Always look for opportunities to be more concise with your writing.

Over time, you'll get more comfortable with your own brand voice and concision.

Tip 8: Always Lead with the Reader First

You want to showcase your expertise and make a positive impression on your followers. That's especially true on that valuable home page real estate, where you have such a short time frame to share your story and connect with the reader.

As mentioned earlier, go back and take a look at your work a second time around. You'll spot things that are you-centric or company-centric or world-centric that don't really speak to the reader's main pain points. Revise your website copy to put the focus on the reader's needs instead.

At the end of the day, you're not the hero of the story. The more you focus too much on yourself or your company story, the more likely it is you don't convince your reader that you're the right choice. Position yourself as a problem solver for your reader.

Tip 9: Don't Get Personally Attached to What You Think Will Work

Even if you've long been told you have a great way of connecting with customers and persuading people with words, you can't get personally attached to your website copy. As with all things digital marketing, it's about strategically making your best estimate and then watching the data to adjust your results. This means the website copy you thought would perform at a high level might end up tanking with low views, people leaving the page quickly, or low conversions.

While this can be frustrating, don't take it personally. Remember that this is actually a very valuable lesson, and you can quickly adjust your content based on this data.

Tip 10: Go Easy on Promotion

If everything feels like clickbait these days, it's because a lot of it is. But the last thing you want is for a reader to feel like they're being pushed to buy, buy, buy the minute they click over to your website.

Tip 11: Don't Oversell Results

If it sounds too good to be true, it probably is. You might feel like your product or service can change your reader's life. But unless that's actually the case for 80 percent of your clientele, leave those grandiose claims out of the picture.

Consider these two statements about a baby sleep coach:

Your world will never be the same again. Finally, your baby will sleep through the night every night because of my proprietary formula! You'll never look back and your life will improve by 200 percent just because of this one small change.

As a sleep coach, it's my goal to help you get more Zs. Your baby needs the sleep, too. I use my proven formula (just ask the 392 parents I helped last year!) to help you create a custom bedtime strategy that works even when you've got a fussy baby.

At face value, these two statements might look similar. But in the second, the writer is relying on outside evidence, not grand claims. This sleep coach feels warm and trusting. This kind of information encourages the reader to do some digging around on the site to find out more about this provider.

Landing pages, sales pages, and actual ads are the best places in your content marketing funnel to build in more promotional opportunities. (More on these later, in Chapter 11.) Take those opportunities, but don't make your entire website seem like a flashing neon sign about your offers.

Tip 12: Focus on Quality, Not Quantity

It's easy to get caught up in the pressure to produce something new every week or every other week. If you don't have a good system for content creation, your work gets sloppy. It's tempting to push out something that seems good enough, but always err on the side of quality rather than quantity. Yes, it's important to teach search engines how regularly you post things, but you don't want to lose all the hard work you've already put in by pushing out content that doesn't meet your basic quality standards.

Tip 13: Create a System for Consistency

If you don't enjoy the writing process or if you're planning to use other writers from Day One, you need a system to ensure your brand voice is used consistently. This can include branding guidelines and checklists. If no rules are in place, things quickly become sloppy and unclear, which can impact the reader's experience.

Tip 14: Remember Accessibility

Not every person who visits your site will have the same abilities. You want your site to have a nice clean design no matter what, so no flashing text or strange color combinations. But don't forget about making your website content accessible. Check out w3.org from W3C for more advice on how to review your own site for accessibility.

Creating Brand Editorial Guidelines

Now that you know your brand UVP and best practices for copywriting, it's time to create some guidelines for consistency across the words you add to your website.

Whether you're writing the content on your own or outsourcing it, keep everyone on the same page by developing brand guidelines. It's normal to feel like you're still finding your voice when you first launch a website project. You might not fill in every aspect of your writing guidelines when you first launch, but return to it over time. The main goal of brand guidelines is consistency. As your company grows or employees change, the brand voice on your website and throughout your marketing materials should stay relatively consistent.

The editorial guidelines for your brand should not be created by one person alone. Build your editorial guidelines with the idea that someday you'll outsource some of your content writing. You want your instructions to be clear and concise, so either a freelance or an in-house content writer can quickly grasp what you hope to accomplish. If you ever work with a proofreader or copy editor, you'll want them to use the writing guidelines as a checklist.

Here are some questions to evaluate as you brainstorm your first round of editorial guidelines:

- How would I describe the overall tone of my brand voice? (Examples include professional, light, witty, or sarcastic.)
- Do I prefer a specific style guide (such as AP or Chicago) for addressing formatting concerns?
- Are there any words or concepts I don't want reflected in my brand?
- What are the "must-haves" for high-quality content published on my website? (Every piece of content should include these items before it's published, such as a recap section, FAQs, clear how-to explanations, or other things specific to your brand.)
- How do you want writers to handle citations and use of other resources? Are certain resources preferred? Are any prohibited (such as competitor content)?

Editorial Guidelines Example

The following is an example of editorial guidelines for Susan, a money and law of attraction coach. She used these guidelines to write her own website content, and she can also share them with her entire team to ensure future writers or social media managers are on the same page with what's most important to Susan and her audience. You'll notice that some of this content includes words from actual clients, reminding Susan and her team of what clients want and need from her.

In order to create content directly in line with what has worked for Susan in the past, she and her team should spend some time evaluating past reviews and client comments. They may find trends in this data that can help them on future projects, using what has already worked for the company. If the company is new and doesn't have this information yet, use a competitive analysis to determine what makes your company unique

Why People Are Drawn to Her and How She Is Perceived at First	Why They Stay
Magnetic and energetic	Internal shifts that led to outward results
Natural, real, caring	A real system/method/consistency in place. *Method* is a word that popped up a lot.
Intentional/method	Community
Luxurious	Personal touch

FIGURE 4.1: **What Attacts Readers and Buyers to Susan**

in the marketplace and why someone would choose your company above another (see Figure 4.1).

Biggest Client Pain Points and Questions

I've done this before, so how will this be different? The investment is huge, so how do I know I will get results?

- ↗ The concept of manifesting or law of attraction is not new to these clients. They really do believe and want the "other way" of existing. Susan's crowd tends to think "I've tried this concept before, and for some reason I still can't crack it." This leads to why should they choose *Susan* to learn from? How will she provide a different experience? Marketing messaging should subtly differentiate Susan from other money experts.
- ↗ "To understand why some people are successful and others struggle." This is what one client said they were looking for before working with Susan. Likely they discovered it's not their job to worry about the how but to tap into the next level for themselves!

I've worked with other people and never got access to them. Actual client quote: "Susan feels like a person, not like those who get your money. She actually reaches out to people."

Many money coaches project the positive aspect/vibe/luxury life well. That's the baseline for this industry. That means for Susan to stand out, she needs to do more than simply project this vibe.

Other people might mirror clients' limiting beliefs and issues, but these clients haven't yet realized that the problem is their own limiting beliefs. They might attract toxic people parroting these limiting beliefs into their world without knowing it, but some of them are also aware of a disconnect in their vibe between what they want to believe with their abundance and the way that plays out in their current mind and real life.

Once you know your client pain points, weave this into your editorial guidelines. For example, Susan's clients want someone who is authentic and also relatable. Even though Susan has achieved great success financially and otherwise, she coaches people about money and needs to strike a balance between sharing her success and allowing it to come across as though it's impossible for others to achieve. She might use what she has learned in this exercise to create editorial guidelines like this:

> Always highlight that while results may not be typical for everyone, doing the work every day and focusing on a new money mindset is possible for everyone. Be realistic in your word choice about what's involved in improving someone's financial situation, but don't make them feel ashamed about wherever they are in starting such a journey. Avoid using terms or phrases that make the person feel like their situation is their fault, that they're to blame for many bad decisions, etc. Instead, focus on the positive future ahead with reframing beliefs and habits.

These guidelines help team members, and especially outside writers, to remember what's most important for Susan to connect with her clients: being authentic, but also not shaming them for whatever situation has prompted them to seek coaching on money issues.

Content Cores for Brand

Essence: Susan as a thought leader and community leader

Core concepts are groupings of words that identify different aspects of a brand. These words also epitomize how a company's clients refer to their experiences of working with them. For Susan's brand, these core concepts are identified as:

- Celebration
- Community
- Evidence and results
- Genuine/authentic
- A proven system

What follows are specific examples of benefits Susan's clients have said they've gotten from working with her, taken from interviews and cases studies. Collectively, these details help make up the core concepts of Susan's brand. This set of brand guidelines includes specific reviews from clients, as well as useful descriptive words and words writers should avoid.

Celebration

Susan's ideal clients are a community that loves to celebrate one another. Not long after someone posts a win in the Facebook group, others are not only happy for this person and chime in to celebrate, but they also see this as evidence that Susan's teachings work.

- Feeling deserved and worthy
- Tapping in to real desires
- Defining an ideal day
- Being open to receive more
- Living life
- Fine-tuning a specific area of my life
- Maximizing my potential
- Loving myself
- Personal freedom
- Manifesting whatever I want
- Being grateful

- Success/manifestation
- Feeling lighter

Community

- "This group of people I am surrounded with only has love."
- "I'm right where I need to be."
- Testimony of gratitude
- "You might not even realize that you're the only person in your life who feels this way or cares about solving this particular problem."
- Feeling like they were trying too hard on their own
- Money family

Evidence and Results

- Manifestation at work
- Seeing the evidence
- Just got a big piece of evidence
- Quick results with Susan: "Susan helped me shift faster than I knew what was happening."
- Specific reactions to results from working with Susan:
  - Ridiculous
  - Amazing
  - "I get excited to wake up and see the chapters and comments."
  - "Out of nowhere"
  - Proof
- Other words to use:
  - Belief/believe it
  - You'll see this showing up everywhere in your life.
  - Quick shifts
- Words not to use:
  - Guaranteed
  - Easy
  - Fast

Genuine/Authentic

Everything in the brand stems from who Susan is—in her marketing, on a daily basis with her, in her emails, and so on.

- Susan has lived the system.
- She can be trusted.
- She actually shows up to help people on live calls. She promises support, and she follows through with it.
- Other words to use:
  - Real
  - Genuine
  - An actual person
  - Living proof
  - Been there before and remapped a new way of thinking for herself first. One client shared their experience as a "180-degree change on life," and this is very similar to Susan's own shifts.

A Proven System

Susan unlocks receiving, results, and freedom for her followers.

- Let go of things that aren't serving me.
- Stop the struggle.
- Before Susan: Why doesn't it work for me?
- Best and most effective ways.

Here again is another opportunity to weave this information into editorial guidelines. These could be reframed into a series of instructions for writers, including guidelines like:

- Always focus on the positive future ahead and the fact that Susan didn't have advanced degrees, money training, or expert financial knowledge when she got started, either. The idea is to make her work accessible to everyone of all backgrounds, no pre-requisites required. Show the concept of hope and new opportunities even for people facing serious financial challenges like bankruptcy.
- Meet people where they are at. When writing, it's OK to call out the fact that many people struggle with money both internally and externally. It's good to reference that they might have tried other things like positive affirmations, debt consolidation, or reading books on the matter, but it might not have worked. Avoid statements/words that could make someone feel more guilt, shame, and blame for themselves.

Chapter 4 Action Steps & Takeaways

- Remember that the best content speaks to your target audience without being overly promotional or you-focused.
- Write original content for your website.
- Proofread.
- Ensure there's a focus to each web page you create.
- Create content with accessibility in mind.
- Create editorial guidelines for your brand.

CHAPTER 5

Understanding Your Buyer's Journey

The cornerstone of great website copy is in knowing the purpose of the website and the basic structure of its pages. In this chapter, we'll address the buyer's journey first, and then we'll explore how buyers move through the marketing funnel to make a decision to purchase from you.

Mapping a Buyer's Journey

Your buyer's journey is an explanation of the process through which your buyer becomes aware of you, evaluates your product or service, and then decides whether to purchase it. This process could take anywhere from a few minutes to years, depending on the product and your industry.

CONTENT IS KING

The first step of building your content marketing strategy is to understand how a customer learns about and commits to your product. A buyer's journey is the steps and the time it takes for them to recognize their problem, discover you, and make the decision to work with you.

It's your job to quickly and clearly communicate who you are and what you're all about to anyone who lands on your website. You can't count on every reader to click through to read everything on the entire site, which is why home page design and user experience are so important.

In the book *Building a StoryBrand*, author Donald Miller explains the marketing concept of the hero's journey. All too often, business owners make themselves the heroes in their website content. To the client, it can sound as though the business comes in to save the day for the client or customer. But, as Miller points out, the company should position itself as a guide to the real hero, the customer. The customer is the one who benefits from completing the journey with the help of the expert guide.

This means you can and should showcase your expertise and your process, but only in a way that shows how that expertise and process will get results for your customer.

Buyer Journeys for Existing Businesses

If you're an existing company, you probably have access to the kind of data you'll need for this exercise. This information is also known as your buying cycle. Some customers have very short buying cycles, while others might extend over months. Take a look at the data you already have about how long it takes your average customer to purchase something from you. This might be a number, such as average months on your email list before they buy or enroll in something. Or it could be the number of touch points your average customer has before doing business with you. If you use a customer relationship management tool such as HubSpot, for example, you can see the average number of emails or phone calls it takes for someone to become a customer.

It has long been said that people need to see or hear about your product or service multiple times before they're ready to buy from you. Given the quantity of ads we see on a daily basis, it's likely that number has increased in recent years.

Imagine you discover in your research that most of your buyers follow your company on social media for six months and open 18 of your promotional emails before buying from you. The first task from here is to see if there's any way to speed up that process. Dig deeper into the data to learn whether any common things tend to tip the scale. For example, maybe you learn that people buy from you after they read three testimonials from previous customers. With that knowledge, you can try eliminating some of the extra email content and targeting more of your social media shares to what is most relevant for your audience.

In some cases, you might not be able to speed up how soon a potential customer does business with you. Lawyers are a great example here, because they have very long buying cycles. Customers might spend months researching possible solutions, whether that's a solo lawyer or a major law firm, before making a commitment. Armed with this knowledge, you, the lawyer, consider ways to speed that up, but you might discover that your audience just needs that long to feel confident in their purchase decision. Your job then becomes finding ways to fill your pipeline so that you always have someone at the top of your marketing funnel (see "How to Understand Customer Movement through Funnels," later in this chapter). If it takes an average of six months to get someone to become a customer, then you should always be marketing both to the people who have already been in your world for six months and to those who are just learning about you, which allows you to build that trust over the next six months.

Buyer Journeys for New Businesses

You can learn a lot by researching your competition and your general industry to discover more about your customers' buying cycles. As a new company, it's very possible that your customer buying cycle will be longer than those of existing companies. From the customer's perspective, you're not a "proven" business yet. You might not have the kinds of marketing collateral of an existing business (such as tested advertising copy, brand awareness, or testimonials from previous customers). Budget extra time and set up ways to capture this data as soon as possible, such as with a customer relationship management tool (CRM).

Create a Visual Map of Your Buyer's Journey

A helpful way to look at the data you've gathered about buyer journeys is to map it in a visual format. This will help you better understand your client overall. It will also help you tailor your content marketing strategy to target certain types of content directly to a specific position in the buyer's journey.

The buyer's journey map is a visual representation of all a customer's interactions with your brand. This is a great way to see where you might be lacking in your content marketing strategy and in your storytelling. For example, if people drop off in engagement at a certain phase, you can tweak your strategy there. You might also learn more about new features or offers that most appeal to your audience, based on what's happening in real time.

Start by listing all the touch points your company might have with a potential customer. This includes your social media channels, your website, interaction at in-person events, or relationships between potential clients and people on your marketing and sales teams.

From there, break down where each of your buyer personas is most likely to engage with your brand. An older demographic of potential customers might become aware of you through a friend's personal recommendation, while a younger buyer probably discovered you on social media or might buy from you through their phone. All this valuable data informs what kinds of marketing campaigns you could direct to those buyer personas to make it a good experience. You might write blogs with product reviews and how-tos for that older audience, while also capitalizing on the younger demographic's desire for instant results by creating content on how technology makes your process incredibly easy.

Customer expectations are constantly changing. That means you need to start mapping your ideal customer's journey and tweaking your findings as you collect data. Data gathering is an ongoing process.

Defining your buyer's journey has benefits beyond your UVP and content marketing strategy, too, such as:

- Helping you figure out how to create a better onboarding experience
- Creating metrics for your sales team to work and set goals from

➤ Better understanding the needs of your customer at each stage of that buyer's journey

Pro tip: One major trend in marketing that influences your buyer's journey no matter the age of your company or industry is humanization and personalization. People see so many ads and pieces of content on a daily basis, and they don't want to be treated like a number. In fact, 84 percent of customers say that being treated like a human has a huge influence on their buying decision. Every time you create personalized touch points for your buyer personas, you increase your chances of successfully getting their business.

How to Understand Customer Movement Through Funnels

Much of marketing is described as a funnel. The funnel refers to the size of your audience as you build a relationship with them and move them from discovering you to the stage of making a purchase decision or becoming a loyal customer. At the top of your funnel your audience size is the biggest because you're not asking much of your audience at that time. Not all of these people will make a purchase. You can break your content strategy into three main pieces here: top of funnel, middle of funnel, and bottom of funnel. More on these in a minute. You might have different strategies within these phases based on your buyer personas. If your marketing materials are not properly aligned to the audience's position within your funnel, you may miss an opportunity to connect and move potential customers further down the funnel.

Consider your funnel like this: At the top are the people who are just beginning their search for information. The next level down are people who are learning about products, followed by those who are reading reviews and checking out competitors. The further down the funnel you go, the smaller the group of people who travel to that level as potential customers. It's your job to use your website and other content marketing to give them the information they need to make a decision and build trust with you, so those customers move further down the funnel toward a purchase.

As you read further, you'll see how you might direct your main website content to appeal to people in any stage of the funnel, while certain types of content such as lead magnets, case studies, or blogs might be directed to people at a very particular point.

Top of Funnel: Awareness or Introductions

The top of the funnel is the awareness stage. When someone first learns about you or your solution, they're not ready to be sold on you yet. This is where people are looking for resources and answers on a topic. Opinions, guidance, insight, and education are most important to buyers in this phase.

Don't send information that's better geared toward those in the middle or the bottom of the funnel to people at the awareness phase. For example, don't write an excellent educational article that meets your top-of-funnel buyer where they are but then closes with a lot of high-pressure sales statements.

Middle of Funnel: Building a Relationship

In the middle of the funnel, followers are evaluating. They started their research process at the top of the funnel, and now they're diving deeper to see whether your product or service suits them and aligns with their needs. You can expect that they are also researching your competitors during this phase, so it's extra important that your content marketing connects them with what makes you unique.

Bottom of Funnel: Purchase Decision

At the bottom of the funnel is where all your hard work pays off with your audience. You've done the legwork to prepare them to buy. At the bottom of the funnel, your audience is in the purchase stage, gathering final details and deciding whether to become a customer.

Once you know who your customer is and where they are at in their purchase decision, you can align your website content with that location. Your readers are more likely to feel an authentic and meaningful connection with your business when you've taken the time to understand their needs, fears, and wants in solving a problem.

As you continue growing your website as a marketing hub for your business, reflect back on the funnel locations for various readers. You may direct certain emails, ads, and blog posts directly at people who are at the top, middle, or bottom of the funnel. Your goal remains the same: to give them the information most helpful to them at that point in time, ultimately moving them further down the funnel toward a purchase decision.

Chapter 5 Action Steps & Takeaways

- ⚐ Consider and map your buyer's journey.
- ⚐ Understand how customers move through funnels and how your website content might fit into that journey.

Outlining and Drafting Your Website Copy

Y ou've figured out your UVP and what your clients want. You
know your audience and how they'll connect with your site.
The next step is to plan and create all that content.

Creating Your Website Content Writing Process

Too many writers attempt to complete huge pieces of their work
all at once, putting something like "write website content" on
their to-do list and then letting it sit there day after day. That's an
overwhelming project. You'll be much more likely to complete the
job when you break it down into smaller subtasks.

Every page of website content you create should have a specific
process. If you are mapping out your entire website from beginning
to end, you might do certain steps of this process together rather

than individually for each page. Start by creating the title of the page and the relevant keywords you hope to mention on that page. (We'll cover keywords in more detail later.) Evaluate your keyword list. Do any terms overlap too much for them to make sense? Will any grammatically awkward keywords be difficult to fit into the content? Which keywords won't drive high-volume traffic or are so competitive it will be difficult to track for and rank them over time?

Next, decide on the primary purpose or action step of each page. Every page on your website should have a goal. Here are some examples of goals:

- To build trust in your products or services
- To explain a complex process
- To inform the reader about the steps they should take in their situation
- To show the reader you deeply understand their needs and concerns

After reading a piece of content on your website, your reader should either feel a particular way or feel compelled to complete a very specific action. For example, on your about page, you might hope the person walks away with a clear understanding of your people-first, innovation-second company culture. This should make the ideal reader comfortable that they have made the right choice in partnering with you. While they might not take action by clicking or enrolling in a call directly from the about page, they should leave with a clear intention.

The reason for naming these goals at the outset of your process is so you can measure against them after the fact and decide whether you've succeeded.

Template for Building Website Page Content

You might continue to refine your company's UVP and brand personas over time, but you can use the template in Figure 6.1 on page 71 to build each individual page of your website. You might come back to this template over the course of several days, filling in details as you go.

Purpose of content	
Name of page/title	
URL	
Main keyword (You'll learn more about keywords in Chapter 7.)	
Target length	
Internal links to use	
External links to use	
Where is the reader psychologically when they land on this page?	
What do I want them to know or feel when they finish reading this page?	
What aspects of a certain persona, if any, do I want reflected on this page?	
What aspects of our story, if any, should be a top focus on this page?	
What is our call to action, if any?	

FIGURE 6.1: **Website Page Content Template**

HEAR FROM THE EXPERTS

EXPERT: AMY RAGLAND

Background: I've worked full time as a freelance marketing writer for nearly five years. Prior to starting my writing business, I worked in corporate communications and marketing for almost a decade and freelanced part time for 15 years.

I create a page overview for every page of the site. Each page overview basically consists of a brain dump of what info the page needs to contain,

EXPERT: AMY RAGLAND

calls to action, downloads or resources the page will need, and any other details I can think to include. I also include notes about possible links to other pages within the site.

Then I get organized. I make a checklist, breaking each page down into smaller copywriting tasks. My checklist might include tasks such as:

1. Write main copy.

2. Write CTA.

3. Write freebie or download offer.

4. Write copy or captions for graphics.

I work through the tasks, checking each one off as the copy is completed and then moving to the next page. As I write copy, I also try to give the design team a clear idea of what's in my head. I'll leave notes throughout the document (usually via comments) if I see certain copy laying out as an infographic. Or if I think we need to start a new section on the page, I'll make a note. I try to think through flow and how to make things as interesting as possible, whether that's through punchier copy or more graphics. That process helps avoid web pages that end up as big ol' walls of text. (Boring.)

Additionally, as I'm writing, I like to keep the site visitor avatar right in front of my face. What information are they looking for when they come to the site? What do they want (or need) to know? How can I make this site a useful resource for them? What copy can I write to make the site more interesting?

Too many companies see a website as simply a place to dump information about themselves, just a web version of a print brochure. I want to make it a place that customers and prospects can come back to whenever they have questions or need to find an answer to a problem.

How to Outline a Website Content Page

Step 1: Write Your Home Page

I've previously referred to your home page as your welcome mat. It's also the first place most new visitors will likely see on your site. Because the home page must appeal to both people who have been there before and those who haven't, you need content that makes it easy for past viewers to navigate to what they're looking for and a layout that shows all you have to offer new readers. This is partly about content and partly about the layout of your site.

Your home page, like the other pages on your site, will include the buttons of a navigational menu either along the top, side, or bottom. The purpose here is to make it easy for someone who is looking for something specific to take the next step.

If you're an aesthetician, for example, your navigational menu might offer people options such as learning more about you, services you provide, a contact form, and a booking page. Keeping it relatively simple is better than making things too complex.

Every page of your website should have one clear call to action. What action step do you want your reader to take after consuming that content? The call to action should be aligned with where your audience is in the decision-making process. For example, someone who is just researching options might not necessarily be ready for a phone call with you. A better call to action for an educational blog post might be another related article.

Your home page can be the hardest part of your site to create in terms of a call to action, because you don't want to overwhelm people. When someone visits your home page, you want them to encounter a solid visual experience that drives them to the most important action they could take at that point in time.

Your home page might not have a lot of text on it at all. For instance, you might include some content about why the reader should click on your call to action, along with white space and an image. But the end goal is the same as any other home page: Don't overload the viewer with information, and get them to click the primary call to action button.

Here are a few questions to consider as you brainstorm your home page content:

- What is the strongest message rather than the biggest collection of messages I can share with my audience on my home page?
- How can my home page quickly and clearly introduce who we are and what we do while leading the reader to the next most important step we want them to take?

Here is a simple visual formula to help you create a great home page:

Navigation Bar
Catchy Opening Statement
Ways You Help People
Introduction to You
Invitation to Follow You or Connect with You
Feedback or Achievements of Note
Footer

Let's talk about each of these sections.

Navigation Bar

Your navigation bar helps your reader easily move around the site.

Figure 6.2 contains an example from my own site— the navigation bar from my "hire me" page. You can see how each of the links is only one or two short words. This makes it easier for someone to navigate to what's most important.

FIGURE 6.2: **Navigation Bar Example**

Catchy Opening Statement

Your opening statement should get your audience's attention. Figure 6.3 on page 75 contains another example from my own website. Your opening

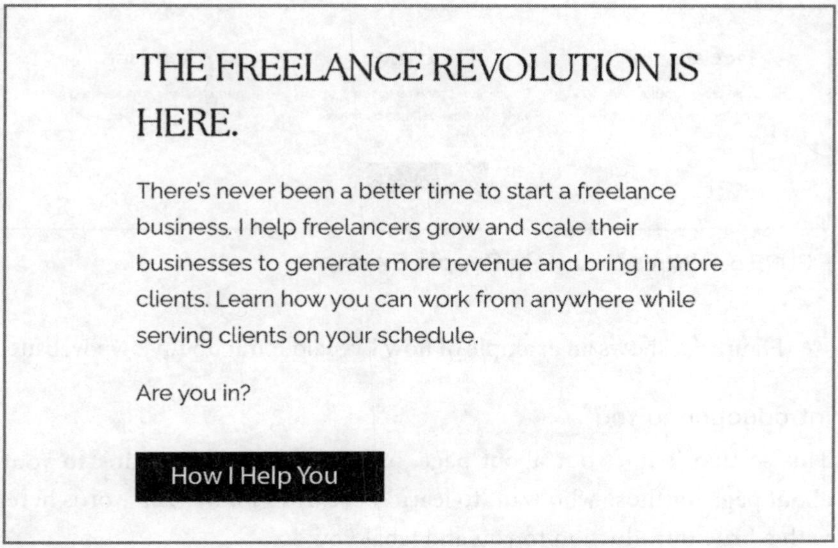

THE FREELANCE REVOLUTION IS HERE.

There's never been a better time to start a freelance business. I help freelancers grow and scale their businesses to generate more revenue and bring in more clients. Learn how you can work from anywhere while serving clients on your schedule.

Are you in?

How I Help You

FIGURE 6.3: **Catchy Opening Statement Example**

statement could simply be what you do, such as "Innovative Marketing Coach" or "Creative Glass Artist" or "Contemporary Interior Designer." Remember the list of brand values we covered in Chapter 3? You can use those adjectives to help you decide what to include in your opening statement.

Or you can look for something more unique that really explains what you do, such as in my example.

Ways You Help People

Most people use this section to explain their offerings. It could include links to other pages on your website, such as:

- Products
- Services
- Coaching
- Speaking
- Hire Me
- Coupons

FIGURE 6.4: **Ways You Help People Example**

Figure 6.4 shows an example of how I've laid it out on my own website.

Introduction to You

This section is not your about page, but you can include a link to your about page for those who want to learn more. Aim for 50–125 words here, with a brief introduction to you and what you do.

Invitation to Follow You or Connect with You

Because your reader will be partway down the page before they see this information, now is a good time to remind them of the best way to connect with you. That could be through an email newsletter, social media, or your contact form. You'll learn more about these options later, when we discuss content marketing that takes your website to the next level.

Feedback or Achievements of Note

Before getting to the end of your site, it's nice to have something that gives you credibility beyond what you've said about yourself. If you have testimonials from people who have liked your work, include a few of them here (a scrolling feature moving through them is impactful, too). If you've won awards, served a high volume of people, or reached other major achievements, close out your site by calling attention to those.

Footer

Your footer recaps some of your most important links, and it also provides details about your privacy policy and the terms of your website. Figure 6.5 on page 77 contains an example of the footer on my website.

FIGURE 6.5: **Footer Example**

Step 2: Write Your About Page

Research from Shopify has found that customers are most likely to navigate to an about page in an effort to learn more about the people and the brand behind the product. This means you need to address these two primary curiosities. Some of the details you might cover in your about page include describing the customers your business serves, communicating the story behind the business and why it was started, and putting a face to the business. Persuasive content, such as an explainer video or links to more blog posts that showcase your story, can be incorporated in the about page when they do not make sense on the home page. The about page can be difficult to write yourself. In fact, many professional writers even outsource the crafting of their about page. If you're feeling stumped by this, it's a good opportunity to reach out to a freelance ghostwriter if you feel overwhelmed. It is very difficult to write things like bios and about pages because they require you to be as compelling as possible about yourself, something that is not always easy to do.

Tips for Brainstorming Your About Page

Although you'll focus your home page on telling the story of the customer on the hero's journey, now is the opportunity to position yourself as the expert guide who will support your customers throughout the journey to their transformation. One of the most compelling ways to do this is to talk about why the company started. Perhaps you felt competitors were missing an important component of the solution, perhaps no solution existed at all, perhaps modern life inspired the need for this particular solution, or perhaps you worked for another company that was not telling this story in the way you wanted.

Turn to the techniques of fiction writing to help you craft your about page. Start by setting the scene and explaining what things looked like before your company began, and introduce the problem that encouraged you to take action. You can then navigate into how you went about determining a solution and starting the business and some of the obstacles you've faced along the way or the early accomplishments you've achieved. As you close out your about page, talk about what's next for you or the company and its goals.

Here's a quick template for an about page:

- A few sentences about who you are at a high level
- How you got into this field
- Why you're passionate about what you do
- The unique approach you bring to the table

About Pages for Bigger Companies

One way to make your about page do more for you is to infuse personality into it. If you're writing an about page from the perspective of the entire company, you might focus more on the organization and its history, but you can also talk about the founders' vision and mission.

One strong positioning statement for a bigger company is that the company has likely grown because of its success. Capitalizing on the power provided by your team and how you're all united by a common mission can speak especially well to one of the downsides of being a bigger team, too, which is that sometimes customers don't feel as much personalization. To combat that, make things personal and show the human side of your company!

About Pages for Smaller Companies

For a solopreneur or a smaller business, focus as much on the people as you can. As a small company or even a company of one, you have a bigger opportunity to make an impression with your followers. Lean into your personal background and how it led you to where you are today. Even if you have a small team, you can talk about the expertise each member brings to the company and how that ends up serving the best interests of clients.

As a smaller company, you're much more likely to connect with your followers through your own perspectives as individuals. Lean into this.

Key Questions to Help You Write Your About Page
- In one sentence, who is your ideal customer?
- What is the mission you're trying to achieve, personally and as a company?
- How do you help other people achieve their goals?
- Why should someone work with you and not your competitors?
- What are one to three fun facts that make you relatable and interesting to your target audience?

Step 3: Draft Your Services and Other Pages

Next, you need pages that explain what you do or how your service benefits your end readers. This is where you do more of a deep dive into the specifics of your offerings.

Questions to Consider When Drafting Services Pages
Each person's services will be unique, but a few common themes tie them together. Consider these questions as you write out how your service helps your target customer:

- Why are you able to get the results you do? (What is your UVP?)
- Why are you the right person to help your clients with their primary pain point?
  - In this section, you'll explain that you understand their pain. Have you been there before? Were you inspired by going through this personally, or with a family member or friend?
- What process do you use when meeting a customer who has a pain point you can solve?
  - How do you break down what might seem overwhelming or overloaded and make it accessible or even enjoyable?
- Why do customers love working with you on this process?

Here's an example from the speaking section of my own website:

Laura Briggs is a 3x TEDx speaker who specializes in bringing together freelancers and the people who need to hire them.

Her keynotes, bestselling books, and online courses have reached over a hundred thousand people interested in the freelance revolution. Her mission is to encourage more people to try out the freelance world, whether for their business or as a business.

All keynotes can be customized for your unique audience and industry. They can be delivered in person or online.

She offers keynotes on:

- *How to leverage freelancers to grow and scale your business*
- *How to get found and get booked by building an online marketing plan that makes you the visible expert in your field*
- *How to scale a service business*
- *How to get more of your time back by hiring a virtual assistant*
- *How to write and publish a book*

Your services pages should be focused on what you do for your readers and how you do it differently. You should give them just enough information to get interested in your offerings while also encouraging readers to connect with you in a deeper way, such as joining your email newsletter, following your social media profiles, or listening to your podcast.

Now you're ready to draft your website content—with your brand values, ways you help customers, and best copywriting principles in mind. Once you've written your drafts, it's time to think about adding bells and whistles, such as SEO (more on that in Chapter 7) and the images you'll use on your site.

Step 4: Proofread and Edit

A fresh pair of eyes the next day or even several hours after writing can help you spot mistakes or assess whether content is still compelling. Your site will also benefit if you hire a freelance proofreader or a marketing expert to get an overall impression of your content. They might point out, for example, that you set out with the goal of creating engaging content, but you spent too much time explaining jargon or sharing information that isn't important to a reader visiting that page for the first time. Take feedback from others with a grain of salt. If it's someone with extensive experience either as a member of your target market or creating content material for your target market, listen carefully. The opinion of an Average Joe, however, who does not have extensive experience with your target market, should be evaluated much less seriously than an expert.

See Figure 6.6 for a checklist you can work through with each page of your website copy and content.

Once you've had a chance to draft your pages, review your work using the following checklist:

☐ My content educates rather than sells.

☐ My content is relatable.

☐ I've avoided using all caps.

☐ My content is unique.

☐ Each page of my site has a clear beginning, middle, and end.

☐ My content has been proofread for grammar and spelling issues.

☐ I've read my content out loud for concision and looked for ways to cut things down.

☐ My content is reader first.

☐ I'm not attached to what I think will work. I wrote my content based on data and best practices.

☐ Quality first, quantity second.

☐ My brand voice is consistent throughout my content.

FIGURE 6.6: **Copywriting Principles Checklist**

Chapter 6 Action Steps & Takeaways

- Write your home page draft.
- Write your about page draft.
- Write your services pages.
- Read your content out loud after writing it to help with editing.

PART II

CONTENT MARKETING STRATEGY

CHAPTER 7

SEO: Optimizing Website Content

A website should help you connect with and convert your ideal prospects into followers or customers, but a website is only as good as the traffic it receives. The idea of "build it and they will come" does not apply to websites. There's so much competition with an online web presence that you need a full-fledged strategy to get found on the internet. That's where search engine optimization (SEO) comes in.

There's no doubt you're writing for your readers first and the search engine second, but you can't neglect either one if you want to accomplish your content marketing goals. In this chapter, you will learn why a website has to speak to the end reader and to search engines at the same time.

Think about where you start most of your research these days. It's online, right? When you need an answer to a question or want to see a listing of products or sites that address certain niches, you head to Google.

You expect that when you type in "best pool vacuums," for instance, you won't just be greeted with pool vacuums for sale, but that you'll also probably hit plenty of search results telling you how to vacuum your pool, reviews of top options, and what to look for when you're seeking answers.

When I did this search, the search engine served up some offers I could buy right away, followed by two ads. Those ads were paid for by the companies who placed them there. That's one way to get in front of your target audience. But let's scroll down in this hypothetical example and see what shows up underneath the ads.

As I would expect, the search engine shows me articles aligned with my search intent. In this case, review websites come up at the top of the organic (aka non-ad) results. How did these companies get there? By investing in these articles and the rest of their content marketing efforts online. This is search engine optimization.

Both your main website pages and any material you add to your site (such as blogs) should be optimized for SEO whenever possible.

The Value of SEO Traffic

Your primary goal with SEO is to get your website listed on the first page of search results for relevant keywords, as outlined earlier. Many people turn to search engines as a way to get answers to their questions and to find the resources they need. But did you know that 75 percent of users never click past the first page of search results?

If your site is optimized to focus on your specialties and keywords, search engine traffic will be much more targeted and therefore more valuable in terms of website visitors. Targeted search engine traffic converts better. That can mean different things, such as people joining your email list, requesting your service, interacting with a chatbot, or performing another call to action. Consider the fact that someone who is actively searching for a solution product or an answer is much more likely to make a buying decision and therefore likely to convert.

Another reason to optimize your website content for SEO traffic is to set yourself up for the future. Properly written articles and other content pages can continue to deliver traffic for years to come. Those results can snowball and lead to further traffic. SEO traffic builds on itself and its impact is long-lasting. This is especially true when you go back to edit or update old materials.

The third reason to optimize for search engines is because it can lead to more consistent traffic than other channels. You may find success with other advertising or content marketing. But these platforms can have dramatic changes to their algorithms that can suddenly tank all your traffic, while SEO is consistent. It will require some updating, but not as much as, say, Pinterest or YouTube. With properly optimized content, you can expect regular fluctuations and patterns every week, or in consistent seasons.

Fourth, evaluating your entire website for SEO makes it difficult for your competitors to copy your content. You become the first and most authoritative word about a particular topic, which cannot be easily duplicated the way other sources of traffic like a Pinterest pin or a Facebook ad could be.

The fifth reason SEO is beneficial is because it is a passive form of marketing that doesn't require significant ongoing effort. It is certainly true that it takes a while for SEO to kick in and that it does require some updates and optimization after the fact. But with optimization, you'll do most of this work once, and then your traffic will likely be relatively consistent.

What Influences SEO?

Google is the biggest search engine out there, but SEO is designed to help you rank on all search engines. There is no way to know for sure exactly what factors and their associated weight determine what sites will appear on the first or second pages of search rankings. That information is both a secret and an evolving process.

That means website owners have tried a lot of different tactics to get their sites to rank. As one example, when search engine rankings first became a thing worth pursuing, many marketers turned to tactics such as keyword stuffing. Their thinking was that if mentioning a keyword phrase once was good, mentioning it 25 times in one piece of website content was better. This tactic led to a lot of terrible website content that didn't help readers with their actual search intent. And, of course, search engines got wise to these tactics. Now search engines do not reward website owners who try these tricks. Google and other search engines continue to monitor for people trying to game the system instead of implementing best practices throughout their website.

SEO is not a "one and done" game. It requires either becoming knowledgeable about the general requirements for an optimized website or partnering with an agency or SEO expert who can do this for you.

Although we'll never know the perfect formula to get our content to rank on page one, we can make some good assumptions based on the history of search engine rankings that the following factors are influential:

- Posting high-quality website and blog content
- Making sure the title of the content matches the searcher's intent
- Posting new content to your website over time
- Making content scannable and visually organized for digital readers (using subheads)
- Providing additional SEO information such as alt tags on photos, links to other pages on the same website, and links to authority pages off-site

At their core, the static, or nonchanging, pages of your website should all be optimized. These are the pages on your site that are rarely updated, such as the home page, services page, or FAQ page. Static services pages will vary by industry and other factors. A few examples follow:

- An aesthetician might have a services subpage for each of the treatments they offer, driven by keyword research. Subpage names might include Facial Peel, Microdermabrasion, or even specific company or brand names of services.
- A law firm might have pages for each of the practice areas they serve.

⤡ A products-based company might use resource pages instead of services pages, with subpages such as Testimonials or How to Use.

Static pages will stay mostly the same over time, but be sure to optimize them when you first create them.

What Is Domain Authority?

SEO has two primary components, both of which contribute to the concept of domain authority. SEO is first based on on-page optimization, which is the effort you take to ensure that each page of your website is properly optimized for the user experience. The second component is off-page optimization, which has to do with the backlink profile and the overall domain authority of the site.

One of the biggest challenges facing website content creators today is that they primarily focus on on-page optimization. This book focuses on on-page optimization, but the best way to build your site's domain authority is to ensure you are covering both components.

Moz, a marketing analytics company, defines domain authority as a Google ranking score between 1 and 100. The closer you are to 100, the greater your chances of your website ranking high in a search. Multiple factors are included in an evaluation of domain authority, such as the number of total links pointing to your website.

You can check your domain authority for free at Moz. Bear in mind that this is separate from a search engine ranking, because domain authority is a score developed by Moz, not by search engines. This means it is Moz's best estimate as to what Google and other search engines find most important.

You might be asking at this point: Why doesn't Google publish this information? Years ago, Google shared data it called *page rank*. That data essentially showed the quantity and the quality of links to a website to determine its overall authority and perceived value for that site based on a scale from 0 to 10. Page rank is no longer shared with the public, although many experts believe that Google does continue to maintain a private database. The Moz domain authority score is the company's best effort to interpret the different factors that could influence page rank, but keep in mind that this is a relative measure and can vary from topic to topic. So it is most helpful for evaluating how you compare to your direct competitors. Moz's domain authority is a great reference point, but don't get too focused on it.

As with all things related to your content marketing strategy, use domain authority to help tell the bigger story and as a data point when evaluating opportunities for improvement. In general, sites that have a higher domain authority score will be more likely to rank on page one, but because Moz's domain authority only tells part of the story, take this with a grain of salt.

Bear in mind that both Google and Moz share a relatively long crawling schedule. This means how often they send out crawlers or bots to your website to evaluate for new and updated content. Crawling can happen within a few weeks or a few months. That means that after you make site changes, you won't see immediate changes to your Google page rankings or your Moz domain authority overnight.

Many different components influence domain authority, including the age of your website and the number of other websites that have linked to yours. This information, much like Google's ranking factors, is not published, so incorporating these ideas will be your best guess.

Matching Titles to Searcher Intent

Have you ever typed something into a search engine, got strange results, and found yourself quickly hitting the back button? Search engines gather data on the back end to make note of when a piece of content doesn't answer a person's question.

Imagine that you're searching for materials on how to turn your garage into an accessory dwelling unit (ADU) for an elderly loved one, but you get a page full of search results about specific laws for ADUs in other states, people who built their own cabins as ADUs, or reviews of construction companies in your area. While some of that information might be related to your underlying query, it's not really what you were looking for, and search engines want to avoid those kinds of scenarios.

So if you did that search and then changed up your search terms or spent very little time on the pages you did look at, the search engine files that away as a swing and a miss.

What this means for you is that even if you come up with a great idea for a page or a blog title, make sure it aligns with what you're actually talking about, because there's nothing more frustrating than scanning through an entire page only to realize it doesn't match your question.

Scannable Content

Online readers do not read your content from the first word to the last. Many are looking for a specific section and use subheads, bolded words, or other visual cues to find what they need. Longer pieces might even include a clickable table of contents at the top for easier navigation. If you've ever followed recipe blogs, you'll know how annoying it is to read a seven-paragraph overview of the blogger's first memory of trying feta cheese before you get to the actual ingredient list. We want to avoid that experience for readers of your website content.

Here are a few ways to make content scannable for a digital audience:

- Use subheads at least every few hundred words (every hundred words is better).
- Add images to break up long blocks of text.
- Try to avoid having more than five or six lines of text in a paragraph.
- Don't use annoying fonts or font sizes on your website that could make your text hard to read.

SEO and Keyword Basics

When you search for something online, search engines deliver two kinds of results: paid ad placements put there by companies who have bid to have their profile and website show up, and organic search engine results, which are the websites Google has determined best answer the query you entered.

For example, if I enter the keyword phrase "become a lawyer" into Google, the top results are ads or paid placements for law schools. (I can tell because they say "Ad" at the beginning of each one.) If I scroll past the paid placements, however, I see the top organic search results for that query, which focus on steps a person could take to become a lawyer.

CONTENT IS KING

Through keyword research and your content marketing, one of your goals is to show up on the first page of organic search results for chosen keywords. The idea is that you'll get the traffic from qualified leads (aka your ideal clients), and it's then your job to convert those viewers into paying customers on your website.

Keywords are the words or strings of words you hope to target, or words and phrases your target audience will search for, on any given page.

The Difference Between Short-Tail and Long-Tail Keywords

When it comes to keywords, both short-tail and long-tail versions exist. Each have benefits for your website SEO strategy. Use both. Long-tail keywords are more relevant for future content, such as blog posts. Your short-tail keywords are more likely to appear on your static website pages.

In general, SEO keywords can range from single words to phrases or questions. They are all used to inform your website content and increase your search engine traffic. These are an important way to connect with your target audience and to signal search engines about the overall content on your website.

Short-tail keywords might be referred to as focused keywords or broad keywords. These search engine queries are made up of one or two words and usually refer to extremely broad topics. This means short-tail keywords are popular and lots of them exist. It also means many website content creators will target them. Having a short-tail keyword strategy alone, however, will not help you stand out against companies with more longevity in the space.

Long-tail keywords, on the other hand, include three or more words and are targeted at very specific or niche audiences. The term *long tail* comes from the lower volume searches associated with long-tail keywords. Because they are more specific, not as many sites show up in a search for a long-tail keyword. Getting your site discovered through lower volume searches is a valuable strategy, because you rank more quickly. Most companies start by trying to rank for long-tail keywords and, over time, increase their chances of ranking for short-tail keywords.

Many companies mix both short-tail and long-tail keywords to target their content needs. You might use online tools such as the Ahrefs keyword difficulty checker to determine how hard it would be to rank in the top 10 websites for a certain keyword. If you target short-tail keywords, for example, you might find that ranking in the top 10 would be difficult or nearly impossible. Many companies instead choose to build their SEO content strategy by targeting lower search volume long-tail keywords first to gain initial website rankings and credibility, poising them more effectively to rank for those shorter keywords in the future.

Keyword difficulty in many checkers is measured on a scale from 0 to 10 or 0 to 100. The higher the number, the more difficult it would be to get organic traffic for that keyword. The low volume of long-tail keyword searches can work to your advantage, because it can greatly increase your visibility and give you a higher ranking more quickly.

Keyword research tools can also give you a window into the paid cost of ranking for a certain keyword on the ad space. Although organic search engine results are based on many of the factors we've discussed here, some companies choose to target specific short-tail or long-tail keyword results in ad placements that appear above the organic search engine results. You can optimize your marketing dollars by targeting long-tail keywords here, although it's important to remember that most people do not trust advertisements placed above organic search results as much as they do the organic rankings.

When doing keyword research, start with an open mind and collect as much information as you can. Keyword research tools can help you do this work. Each has its own pros and cons. The tools Google Ads Keyword Planner, Ubersuggest, or Keywords Everywhere can be great starting points to help you think about what content is most relevant to your target audience.

How to Use Modifiers with Your Keywords

Using only a list of generic keywords exposes your business to the possibility of never ranking for those keywords. To help increase your chances of ranking, you might add alternative keywords, longer-tail keywords, or keyword modifiers. Keyword modifiers are words added to a search query to specify an additional element of the searcher's intent. For example, there is a difference between searching for "haircutting scissors," "best haircutting scissors," or "cheapest haircutting scissors." *Best* and *cheapest* are examples of keyword modifiers in this case, and they can help you achieve a better connection with your reader, assuming your blog post or services page on haircutting scissors goes far enough to answer their questions.

Geographic Content and Keywords

Nationwide companies will all likely be competing for similar keywords. One way to differentiate yourself as a local business or a brick-and-mortar business is to use geographic keywords.

One of the biggest challenges with this approach is that most geographic keywords are not grammatically correct, which can make them very awkward to write. Your natural instinct as a new website content writer might be to work in geographic terms exactly as they are listed on the keyword search, but this can be an uncomfortable experience for the reader. For example, the keyword might be "car accident lawyer San Diego."

Targeting your content with "car accident lawyer San Diego" and leaving out modifiers such as *best* or *experienced* or the word *in* can make things difficult as you weave this phrase throughout your content. It is essential that you find a way to fit in this keyword in the grammatically incorrect form you found in your keyword research. But once you've done that, you can mix up variations on that keyword phrase throughout your content. Don't try to work in these grammatically incorrect phrases frequently. That can read unnaturally and make your audience question your overall writing ability.

Meta Descriptions, Title Tags, and Subheads

Keywords, along with internal and external links (see more on backlinks later in this chapter), all help to drive the success of your SEO content. But you cannot forget about a couple of important site structure specifics that should be included on every page. The first of these is your meta description. Your meta description should be between 50 and 156 characters, and it helps to explain what the general page or website is about. For your home page, your meta description may be a generic description of what the entire company offers, while an individual page description helps point toward a specific answer or question that piece of content addresses. The meta description should include the primary keyword and give both the search engines and prospective readers a clear understanding of the page's primary content.

The second site structure specific is a title tag. This is a short section of content that helps to explain the primary title of the page you're viewing.

Title tags should always include the focus keyword as close to the beginning of a title as possible. A title that doesn't do this won't specifically harm your user, but using it is a known factor for positively influencing the SEO ranking of that page.

Imagine that your primary keyword is "dog walker Newport News."

Next, imagine your title tag is "Seven Tips for Finding the Best Dog Walker in Newport News." That title works grammatically and it properly explains the content that would follow on that page. However, the primary keyword is too close to the end of the title tag. Thankfully, this is easy enough to fix. Consider "Finding a Dog Walker in Newport News: Seven Top Tips."

As you map out your website pages, the next thing to think about are subheads. Subheads are excellent real estate for incorporating complementary or additional keywords. Every website content page should follow a natural flow.

The primary keyword should be mentioned in the title of the page and in the first subhead, but look for additional opportunities to include those supplementary and complementary keywords, too.

How Much Should SEO Influence Your Content?

Not everything you publish to your website as a blog needs to be directly aligned with SEO. It's fine to work company news or hot topics that your clients always ask about into your overall content rotation. But if you're trying to drive traffic to your website, SEO must be a part of that process.

What Doesn't Need to Be Optimized for SEO?

Investing your time and energy into learning SEO principles as you craft a website is well worth it. However, it's not a strategy you need to apply broadly to all your content marketing efforts. This is because different things are required when attempting to reach audiences in different places.

SEO drives the connection between your website and the search engines, but building a human connection and including hashtags are more important for social media. You wouldn't use hashtags at the bottom of your published website page or blog, so be prepared to adapt and repurpose all your content for the proper medium. Start by crafting website content with SEO in mind, and then adapt the published work for sharing in places like email newsletters or social media.

CONTENT PRUNING AND SITE MAINTENANCE

Because you're just now getting the words on the page for your website, it may feel as though it doesn't make sense to talk about getting rid of content. But it's worth mentioning this now, so you can build content pruning into your regular editorial strategy. Every six months to a year, you'll want to evaluate the performance of the pages on your website and determine which ones should be deleted, updated, or added. This time period allows you to collect data on what's working well. If you have dozens of pages or blog posts on your website by then, you might increase this frequency to once per quarter.

Tools for Keywords and SEO

Plenty of tools can help you check your website pages for optimal SEO. If your site is built on WordPress, the plug-in Yoast SEO will give you traffic light colors to indicate whether you're on track for proper SEO. Don't get hung up too much on things like active vs. passive voice, though. Yoast will give you scores including this factor, but other factors influence SEO more. Simply aiming for a green light per page doesn't mean you're done with SEO. It's simply a guideline to help you proof and edit during your final pass.

Tools such as Clearscope or Frase help you map out an editorial strategy. Both of them make recommendations about length of page and other keywords, if you need that help. These are paid tools and are only worth investing in if you decide that blogging is core to your strategy of attracting readers and followers. You'll learn more about content marketing strategy and blogging in Chapters 8, 9, and 10.

Google Ads Keyword Planner

Google Ads Keyword Planner is a user-friendly tool you can check out to get a better handle on which keywords searchers are looking for and their search volume.

As one example of how to use Google Ads Keyword Planner, I looked at the search term "cleaning out gutters," which might be relevant for a lawn care company's content marketing strategy. When I do that, Google shows me some important information based on my original idea, such as:

- Other relevant keyword strings
- How often that set of keywords is searched each month
- How easy or hard it would be to rank my new page for that keyword
- How much it would cost me to run an ad at the top of the organic search engine results

When selecting keywords, it's tempting to pick the ones that have the highest search results. After all, if 14,000 people are looking for a term every single month, wouldn't you want to target that term first? The answer is no. If you're a new website with little to no traffic currently, you don't yet have what I call search engine credibility. This means you don't have a track record for publishing good content that is SEO optimized. By adding to your website, you're building that credibility.

You'll also be competing with many other sites targeting that same keyword, and those sites might have a better content strategy or a longer history, meaning it will be hard to beat them. If another company has invested months or years into their content marketing, search engines will likely rank multiple pages owned by that business on the first page of results. That company has put work into being seen as a resource hub for people around a specific topic. It's harder as a new website or a company just beginning its content marketing to match that. The best combination is to look for a keyword with decent search volume and low competition.

One paid keyword tool I use is called Keywords Everywhere. Let me describe how it can work. I searched for "best foods for low inflammation" and the tool gives me related keywords I could target. A volume column shows data on how many searches for that phrase happen per month. A CPC (cost per click) column tells me what I'd have to pay to place an ad for that keyword set (which is outside the scope of organic SEO, but it explains the perceived value of that keyword). Finally, the competitive score tells me, from .00 to 1, how difficult it will be to rank for that keyword. A score of 1 means extremely difficult. An initial reaction when viewing this might be to look at the keyword with the highest search volume and say "Wow! That's a great choice because the search volume is high!" However, if my website is new, I likely won't rank for that keyword because it's too competitive. Instead I might first target something a little further down that list, because while it does have search traffic, I'll be able to rank for it more quickly.

Keyword Selection Tools

Tools such as Semrush or Ubersuggest can help you pick the right keywords for your site. What follows is a quick overview of how to use them.

Semrush for Keywords

- Once you're on the Semrush dashboard, go to the Keyword Magic Tool, under the Keyword Research section.
- Then enter a seed keyword (a short-tail keyword with only one or two words) of your choice. Make sure to select the database where your target audience is geographically.
- Now add filters to get a better keyword research process. Click on the Volume filter. Enter from 100, to 1,000, and apply the filter.
- Add another filter of KD (keyword difficulty) to find low-competitive keyword ideas. It's almost impossible to get number-one rankings for most keywords, but you can certainly get top rankings when you go for less competitive keywords.

- Click on any of the keyword terms and Semrush will generate even more keyword data.
- Use the Keyword Magic Tool to find keyword suggestions that include question-based keywords, phrase match keywords, and related keywords.
  - Question-based keywords are long-tail keywords that are becoming more popular and should be part of your SEO strategy. They are extremely helpful if you want to rank for featured snippets on Google.
  - Phrase match keywords are exact keyword terms that match your target keywords. If you are looking for keywords that must include the primary keyword, phrase match keywords can help.
  - Related keywords are those that are similar to your seed keyword.

How to Use Semrush to Find Competitor Keywords

- Under the Semrush Competitive Research section, go to the Organic Research tool. Enter any of your competitors' domains. You will instantly get a list of all the keywords that site ranks for.

How to Use Ubersuggest for Keyword Research

- In Ubersuggest, enter an initial keyword term, and then click View All Keyword Ideas. The tool should generate more than 120 keywords for a target keyword. You can also click on the Related tab to find a list of related keywords.
- The Questions tab is right next to the Related one. It will help you get rankings for featured snippets.
- The Prepositions tab will give you new options.

Backlinks and Off-Page SEO

When another website links to your website or the material shared on your website (known as backlinking), this helps to improve your domain authority and backlink profile. Essentially, another content creator is saying the material you have created on a specific topic is authoritative. This helps to improve your overall SEO rankings. More than 200 factors influence Google rankings, and some of them have to do with your backlinking profile. This means it's not enough to only pay attention to on-page optimization, although that is the cornerstone of your content marketing strategy.

While on-page SEO refers to everything that happens within the site, your off-page SEO amplifies those results. Your off-page SEO refers to all the activities that happen away from your site, such as brand mentions in media features, backlinks, and social media. Together, these components work to help show Google and other search engines that you have an authoritative and high-quality site. Over time, the more backlinks you build in conjunction with your quality on-page SEO efforts, the easier it will be to climb up the rankings.

What Kinds of Backlinks Should I Seek Out?

Not all links are created equal, and simply pursuing a cheap but widespread linking strategy could land you in hot water. If low-quality websites drive traffic and links to your site, that will not give you a higher domain authority score. Here's what you do want:

- Links from sites related to yours in topic area or niche
- High-quality links, such as from sites that already have their own established domain authority rankings
- Diversity of links, meaning not all the links pointing to your website come from the same small number of places

Assess your domain authority by looking closely at the results of your direct competitors. Looking at big players in the internet space will only make you frustrated, so make a short list of your competitors and their current domain authority scores, as well as your own domain authority score if you already have a website. You can find your domain authority by using the moz.com Link Explorer and also use their free Chrome extension to see the page and domain authority for every website you view.

What You Need to Know about Building Internal Backlinks

As noted earlier, external backlinks are another website owner's way of saying your site content is authoritative and search engines should interpret it that way. However, far too many content creators overlook the option to create internal links. Overall, external backlinks do have a much more powerful impact on your overall website credibility and your domain authority score. But along with your other SEO checklist items, internal linking should be at the top of your priority list. Every page should include two internal links to other relevant pages on your website.

For example, imagine that you are an artist providing commission-based oil paintings. On page four of your site, Ordering a Commissioned Oil Painting, you might also link to previous work or feedback from customers. These would be other relevant pages on your website. Readers will be able to identify internal links because your anchor text (the clickable text of those links) will be a different color or underlined.

You can also use the *related* strategy to help drive traffic to other places on your website. Using the example above, perhaps you (the artist) have blogged about your process and the art fairs you have attended. You might use a closing statement at the end of the post that says "see related articles about previous art fairs and awards." This can drive interested traffic to other places on your website. One of the most important things to keep in mind here is that the keyword text should be accurate. You will provide useful information to your readers and keep them on your own site much longer.

Linking Mistakes to Avoid

Black hat SEO techniques, or unethical methods of trying to improve rankings, should be avoided at all costs. These can take down the ranking of your website and decrease its perceived authority. You may see short-term gains from these techniques, but Google will catch on and can punish many different sites at once through a widespread algorithm update. Here are some tips for keeping your site on the up-and-up:

- Avoid paid links. It is against Google's terms of service to pay to have a link placed somewhere. Do not sell links on a highly ranking website and do not buy links either.
- Avoid link exchanges, where someone promises you a link on their site in exchange for links on yours. These involve networks where multiple people are exchanging links, and this, like the above

example, is against Google's terms of service. For the most part, you can expect that other websites involved in networks like this have ranking problems of their own and are not sites you would want to link to anyway.

Don't use link farms or link wheels. These terms refer to a series of websites created with the sole purpose of linking to one target page. This is a way of gaming the system. These are most popular with bloggers in specific niches who create a series of links to one another. Because Google's network can easily spot these linking patterns, it can take down and penalize all sites within the link wheel.

Finally, don't overoptimize your link text. Just as you would avoid keyword stuffing in your content, do not keyword stuff the anchor text, which is the text you use to create links. Once you understand the process of getting backlinks to your site, you might assume it would be easiest to do one massive outreach effort to get as many links as possible pointing back to your site. But that comes across as spamming and is not helpful to the user. For example, you would not need to link to "Colorado personal injury attorney," "personal injury attorney in Colorado," and "car accident lawyer in Denver" all within the same paragraph driving links to different locations. Resist the urge to do this, because Google is wise to this practice as well, and it could end up harming your overall website ranking capabilities.

Chapter 7 Action Steps & Takeaways

- Make sure your static website pages (home page, about page, services pages) are generally optimized for search engines.
- Do keyword research to learn what people might search for in your service area, and use those keywords as naturally as possible throughout your content.
- Make your content easily scannable with optimized titles and headlines.

CHAPTER 8

From Website to Content Marketing Strategy

Your website, as you've currently drafted it, is technically complete once you launch it. Some companies simply want to ensure they've got a website with good design, great copy, and functioning navigation up for the time being. However, to get the most from your website, you'll need to use this launched website as part of a broader content marketing strategy.

What Is Content Marketing Strategy?

A content marketing strategy relies on a few important components to consistently connect with your target audience. The first step is to narrow down your target audience so that you are crystal clear about who you're helping and their biggest needs at the time your content marketing reaches them. If you are not clear about who your target market is, it will be very difficult to connect with them, much less provide relevant information targeted to their needs. Fortunately, you did this work of understanding your audience back in Chapter 3.

The purpose of your content is to connect with potential buyers about their pain points to provide solutions or clear information, which leads into the second component of your content strategy. You're not the first person to have this particular content strategy or content marketing in your niche, and you certainly won't be the last. This means you need to have some sort of competitive edge over everyone else who is also creating similar content. You do this by creating better content than your competitors while still tapping into your audience's pain points. You must be able to present a compelling story that clearly and effectively connects with them. You can only do this when you know your UVP. As you learned in Chapter 3, your UVP is the unique, helpful approach you take to solving your audience's problem. You will constantly be in competition with other people creating content marketing, so creating content is not a one-and-done task. You'll return to it again and again as you audit, delete, update, and create new material.

The third prong of your content marketing strategy is to understand the best ways to reach that target audience. If you are looking for organic search engine traffic, for example, your strategy likely involves a blog component. You might discover that your audience is most active on social media, which means driving content to your website may begin with an organic or a paid social media campaign. Each of these strategies and ways to connect with your potential audience all require knowledge in that area.

The final step of your content marketing strategy is to have a system to return to what you are creating, so you can update material that is outdated or not working and continue to build on your success. Reviewing analytics and carrying out site and content maintenance is ongoing work. Free website analytics tools include Google Analytics, while paid options include software such as Semrush or Ahrefs. In reviewing data for your own website, you'll discover what's resonating and what's performing poorly. A website requires a lot of upfront work to launch, but it's an investment that can pay off in dividends for you in the future. If you put in the work and time with your content marketing strategy, you'll continue to update and add new material to your website, too.

For example, perhaps you discovered in that analysis process that how-to articles are the most effective way to reach your target audience. In that case, a core component of your content marketing strategy could be making sure your how-to articles remain up-to-date and accurate. You might discover that other content performs poorly or isn't getting the traffic you expected. Perhaps that traffic is landing on your page because of a different search intent.

We'll talk more about SEO strategies later on, but here's a brief story about why not all traffic is created equal. I once worked with a company that had thousands upon thousands of ranking website pages and keywords. Some of that keyword traffic, however, was utterly useless.

The company was in the legal space, and it was drawing traffic for searches like "best purses for female lawyers." That certainly got traffic to their website, but it wasn't effective traffic because it wasn't necessarily the people they sought to target. Make sure your content marketing strategy always aligns with the balance of the potential to bring in traffic and the journey your audience takes.

Your content strategy certainly starts with your primary website, but you'll build out from there with other things you do to drive traffic to that site, like a blog.

What Makes Content Strategy Different from Content Marketing?

Content strategy refers to the development, planning, and management of content and other media. Content strategy is the primary purpose that guides your entire effort as a content marketer. It includes the strategy, the guidelines, and the step-by-step process through which you approach content. Content marketing, however, is the actions you take, including brainstorming of topics, creation and publication of content marketing pieces, and the distribution and promotion plan connected to targeted audiences online.

Creating Your Content Strategy

At a broad level, content strategy focuses on the creation, planning, governance, and delivery of content. This goes beyond the words listed on your actual page and incorporates other media elements used to tell the bigger story. The biggest thing to remember is that your goal is to create sustainable, engaging, comprehensive content.

Content strategy helps you accomplish business requirements through the creation and updating of content. Content strategists look at how to achieve business objectives and interests through content creation and develop designs and roadmaps for distributing that content. For more details, check out the book *Content Strategy for the Web* by Kristina Halvorson and Melissa Rach.

The Brain Traffic Model

Content Strategy for the Web uses what it calls the *brain traffic model* to map out the most important elements of content strategy. Following are the five primary components of content strategy:

- *Core*: How will the content be used?
- *Substance*: What content is needed?
- *Structure*: How is that content organized?
- *Workflow*: How is content created?
- *Governance*: How do we decide what to do?

To get started, you'll need to focus on your marketing goals and your capacity to create and implement, beginning with one specific plan. You can, of course, be successful with many different types of content marketing strategies, but failing to commit to a specific plan or overcommitting yourself and then getting overwhelmed are ways to fail.

A content marketing strategy should align with your individual goals and the capacity of your current team. Research from the Content Marketing Institute found that more than 63 percent of businesses don't have a documented content marketing strategy. This makes it difficult for those businesses to regularly execute on content creation and publication. Being intentional about creating content and the formats in which you create it can dramatically increase your chances of connecting with your target customer.

Determine What's Most Important to You

Your content marketing strategy might accomplish more than one aim at a time, but having a core component to measure your efforts against will help you define what's reasonable and what might be a distraction or a future goal. At its foundation, your content marketing strategy should consider your target audience, the content you use to reach them, and the benefits those readers will obtain from connecting with that content. An easy way to do this is to fill in the blanks in this sentence: We create _____ kind of content to help ____ target reader accomplish _____.

You'll also have your own set of website-specific business goals that drive your content marketing strategy, such as getting more traffic to your site, improving your SEO rankings, reducing your marketing overhead, making more sales, getting better engagement on social media, and improving revenue.

Key Performance Indicators

Key performance indicators (KPIs) help you determine what is most effective in your content marketing strategy so you can measure results. Creating content for the sake of creating content will not likely yield any results for you. If you invest months in creating and publishing content without setting KPIs upfront, it will be difficult to tell whether you achieved your goals.

Especially in your early days when you may not have much growth, seeing some movement in the right direction can encourage you to keep going. Furthermore, checking your progress against your KPIs will allow you to make pivots and changes in your content marketing strategy as you see what works and what doesn't. Some of the KPIs you might set include:

- Number of organic page views of your blog per month
- Number of keywords ranking in the top 10 or top three on Google
- Percentage of keywords making improvements month over month

- Increasing email subscribers as a result of on-page visitors
- Better social media engagement
- More podcast downloads
- More sign-ups for your opt-in email list

Defining the Right Content for Your Audience

If your website already exists, you can dig further into your audience's interests by using Google Analytics. Visit Audience, then Interests, and then Overview to see the market segments your current web visitors fit into. You might include a content marketing strategy that sets specific goal numbers for how many pieces of content you'll produce each month in the form of:

- Short blog posts
- Long blog posts
- Social media content
- Podcast episodes
- Case studies
- White papers
- Infographics
- Ebooks
- Videos
- Email marketing, such as newsletters

Content Creation vs. Content Curation

There is a difference between creating content and curating content. Within your content marketing strategy, you'll likely use both. With content creation, you are the one brainstorming ideas. Those ideas might be partly based on research or popular keywords, but you are gathering resources from your personal experience, your company's materials, and elsewhere on the web to create original pieces. This is different from content curation, where you might directly share other people's content on its own or share it with your own brief comments. For instance, sharing your own blog post on LinkedIn or writing a 200- to 300-word short-form piece to educate your audience about your industry is content creation. Commenting on another person's post, sharing their blog post with a few sentences of your insight, or adding to the overall discussion is content curation.

While your primary focus should be on creating your own compelling marketing copy based on the principles in this book, your content marketing strategy will ideally make use of both. The longevity of your created content is much longer than curated content, and it showcases you as an authority and thought leader. That said, don't ignore the possibilities available with content curation. You can connect with other influencers and greatly expand the possible reach of your audience. For example, imagine that a popular nutritionist completes a study on the impact of intermittent fasting. If you are a health coach, you can add to their research results, connect with them on LinkedIn, reference the study and provide a backlink in your blog, and have a much easier time introducing yourself to this other influencer. Building your business by renting other people's audiences is a solid strategy, and in this way, you are not claiming ownership of the material created by the nutritionist but rather amplifying and supplementing it.

How to Determine and Allocate Resources for Your Content Marketing Strategy

Now that you've determined the kind of content you intend to create and how it will reach your target audience, as well as the KPIs you'll use to track your success, let's think about what resources you may need to execute on this strategy. Do not overload yourself with the entire process of developing and creating this content unless you can commit to the time and resources required. For most solopreneurs, this means dialing back the volume of content marketing production to align with what they can realistically achieve. Some of the questions you'll consider as you assess content resources include:

- What digital tools do you need to create content?
- Who will be in charge of producing and updating content?
- Will you need a copy editor or other final proofreader to help keep an eye on minor details?
- What does the publishing process look like, including scheduling and publishing of content?

Content Production Roles

Many factors will influence the creation of ongoing website content, such as the size of your company and whether you currently have an existing content team. If it's just you, you might break this project down into several smaller steps.

If you're not able to produce content in-house, you'll need to develop a budget and a schedule for outsourcing this work. For example, the company's CEO or chief marketing officer will be the one who approves titles and develops the editorial calendar, but you might need to hire a content marketing manager to ensure your strategy is on track from day to day or to manage the rest of your content team. Individual members of your team might develop the content, or freelancers might provide drafts to that content marketing manager.

Remember to include financial details in your content marketing strategy, whether that means paying an in-house person or relying on freelance help or an agency to support you.

You might need help in the form of:

- A freelance writer or in-house writer
- A copy editor
- A content manager, who assigns projects and moves them through the workflow
- An SEO specialist

In Chapter 12, which addresses outsourcing in more detail, we'll talk more about the different people you could hire to help with marketing implementation.

Setting Up a Content Workflow

Developing a workflow will help keep things on track and ensure consistency across your entire brand voice. Your content production process should include steps such as:

- Determining topics and primary keywords
- Creating outlines and getting them approved
- Writing posts yourself or outsourcing them to the person who will write them

- Sending posts to the editor
- Creating accompanying social media images and additional links
- Doing a final pass review
- Making revisions or passing revisions to a freelance writer
- Uploading content
- Publishing content
- Executing on the promotional plan for that piece of content

Chapter 8 Action Steps & Takeaways

- Decide on your content marketing strategy. How will you consistently reach your audience and drive traffic to your website?
- If you choose to use content marketing, how will you track it? Decide on your key performance indicators.
- Verify that you have or will invest in the right resources to pull off your content marketing strategy.
- If you'll be investing the time and resources into ongoing content marketing, what schedule will you use to stay on top of it?

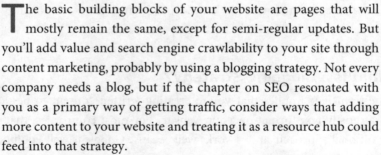

Blogging Basics

The basic building blocks of your website are pages that will mostly remain the same, except for semi-regular updates. But you'll add value and search engine crawlability to your site through content marketing, probably by using a blogging strategy. Not every company needs a blog, but if the chapter on SEO resonated with you as a primary way of getting traffic, consider ways that adding more content to your website and treating it as a resource hub could feed into that strategy.

In this chapter, you'll learn more about the value of blogging, including recommendations on how blogs can drive search engine traffic, how to determine topics relevant to the ideal reader, and how blogging functions differently from static website pages.

Is Blogging Dead?

Every few months I see someone post that *something* in marketing is dead. It might be blogging, SEO, or podcasting. But the truth is that content is king. Whether it's the written word or audiovisual materials you're translating into the written word, you need a way to share your content with your audience.

Regular, high-quality content published to your website really does make a difference. Here are a few statistics that highlight how and why a blogging strategy can pay off for your business:

- According to TechJury, bloggers who publish every day get better search results.
- Google gets 100 billion searches per month.
- Hundreds of millions of blogs are on the web today.
- 77 percent of web readers look at blogs.
- 70 percent of people would rather learn about a company through an article than an ad.

Blogging and other forms of content marketing bring the reader to you. This is powerful, because in some sense many of these readers are already primed. They have a problem, they're looking for answers, and they're trying to find an authoritative source to give them those answers. When you've set up your company as a resource hub with well-crafted content that meets the reader's needs, you can form a relationship with that reader that brings them back again and again.

What Is a Blogging Strategy?

The term *blog* implies that you're creating written content to be posted in a mostly text format on your website. For most companies, that's the traditional approach, and it works well because Google is well-equipped to crawl and understand written content. But since the inception of blogging, the idea of what it means to blog has evolved quite a lot.

So what is a blog? Very simply put, it is an article or short essay. People take different approaches toward blogging. Lifestyle bloggers write personal information about their lives. Recipe and cooking bloggers include a lot of pictures of their meal prep, and they may include backstory about what's happening in their lives or what led them to try a particular recipe.

The History of Blogging

Blogging has been around for a long time in internet years. Justin Hall created the first blog in 1994, although he didn't call it that and simply referred to his text updates as his personal home page. In 1997, Jorn Barger first used the term *weblog*. The first online diary-style option started in 1998, and the launch of the company Blogger in 1999 gave everyone with access to the web a way to share updates and write about things they cared about.

Since then, blogging has become a vital component of any company's content marketing strategy. Although it has evolved from updates or personal perspectives into long-form content marketing designed to capture and convert an audience, it's valuable today as a means of growing your brand. People turn to the web to get answers to their most important questions and to learn about a broad range of things, which is why content marketing is so key.

Simply put, your blogging strategy is part of your content marketing plan to reach your audience on a regular basis with content you have created.

Where Does Blogging Strategy Fit In?

A blogging strategy should work alongside the other content on your website. The primary difference is that much of the other content on your website is created once and updated a few times per year at most.

A blog is the fresh content you add to your website on an ongoing basis. It's probably the content on your site that changes the most, because ideally you should be blogging either biweekly or weekly.

You've already read Chapter 7, so you know the important role SEO plays in getting your website ranked and improving your visibility in your industry. Blogging and SEO are interconnected, so remember to use the results of your keyword research to help drive your editorial calendar.

Every blog post you create will likely go through the same process, from conceptualizing ideas through publication to promotion. Your process might look like the following:

1. Research keyword topics.
2. Brainstorm additional topics with team.
3. Determine whether topics need to align with specific dates, such as holidays or special company promotions.
4. Draft outlines.
5. Write blogs.
6. Edit blogs.
7. Publish blogs.
8. Share on social media or in your email newsletter.

What Makes a Good Blog Post?

As with many things SEO-based, a great blog is about connecting with readers. A good blog:

- Provides helpful information in an easy-to-read format
- Considers its readers' common questions and objections throughout
- Goes beyond basic information readers could find elsewhere
- Positions you as a thought leader in your field

Do I Need to Use Images Throughout My Blog?

Much of this book has been about the text of content marketing, but you can't ignore visuals. Visuals such as infographics or photos can help add creativity to your pieces, back up claims you make, and also break up long blocks of text. Be mindful when using stock photo websites, though. Some sites that claim to provide "free" stock photos might not actually be free to use. Check their terms of use. For example, you might be required to credit the photographer, which can be distracting and unwanted for website owners.

Alternatively, you might choose to pay a commercial stock photo site to properly license images for your site. You can use a graphic creation tool such as Canva to grab those additional elements and infuse them with your personal branding colors and fonts. Building infographics (which you can also do with Canva) is another way to connect with your readers and share excerpts from your bigger blog posts across social media.

Visual Elements of Your Site Pages: Infographics

Infographics combine visual and text-based story elements to share details about a process or relevant research with your audience.

Infographics are usually stored as PDF or JPEG files on your website because they are not completely text based. These can be great tools for getting off-website visitors (like social followers) to come to your site when you share them over other channels. Infographics are elements of pages, not pages themselves. You might host them on a blog or services page.

Because you can put your own unique spin on the content and curated research of an infographic, it's an excellent way to brand your work. You can add your logo, too. Just remember to credit any resources you used to gather information.

Here are some examples of infographic topics different businesses might use:

- An email service provider might create an infographic about best practices in email marketing.
- A book publicist might create an infographic about what goes into a holistic public relations plan for an author, including details about average sales numbers for self-published authors.

How to Create an Editorial Calendar

An editorial calendar makes it easy to choose what to write about and when, removing decision fatigue in the future when it's time to sit down and write a post. Your editorial calendar is essentially a roadmap of your content marketing plan. For most, this will reference planned blog posts, dates when drafts are due, and when the final pieces will publish. For companies using more complex content marketing strategies, this calendar can also include details about other outputs such as infographics (images sharing data visually) or lead magnets (free reports, checklists, and the like), along with email newsletter sends and social media topics. Although not all these things are website content, they are often grouped together with blog posts and podcasts because these pieces of content tend to follow regular and predictable publication patterns.

Let's talk through one hypothetical company, an adrenal healer, and how they might plan their editorial calendar.

For this example, let's assume the healer has created a basic website with a home page, about page, contact form, resources page, and a services page. From these bare bones, the healer could create an editorial calendar based on their highest-priority keywords.

The healer did their keyword research and selected the following keywords:

- Adrenal fatigue symptoms in females
- Adrenal fatigue healing time
- Symptoms of adrenal fatigue
- Fruits for adrenal fatigue
- Adrenal fatigue syndrome
- Adrenal fatigue causes
- Adrenal fatigue test

From this brain dump of possible keywords, the next step would be to determine which ones make the most sense to combine, delete, or prioritize. The fact that both "symptoms of adrenal fatigue" and "adrenal fatigue symptoms in females" appear on this list is helpful, and the company owner could handle this in one of two ways. First, they could create comprehensive blog material for each one, tailoring one of the posts specifically toward symptoms for women.

Or they could use the general keyword ("symptoms of adrenal fatigue") as the primary keyword and first head while including breakdown sections for both men and women to reference the other keyword, too. If you have a hard time finding enough keywords to build out an editorial calendar, or if you find a specific reason to break topics like that into two pieces and can distinguish them enough from each other, I recommend the first strategy.

Using those keywords, we might set up one of the following two editorial calendars:

Simple Editorial Calendar

- Week 1: Blog Post #1, keyword adrenal fatigue syndrome
- Week 2: Blog Post #2, keyword adrenal fatigue causes
- Week 3: Blog Post #3, keyword adrenal fatigue test
- Week 4: Blog Post #4, keyword symptoms of adrenal fatigue

Complex Editorial Calendar

- Week 1: Blog Post #1, keyword adrenal fatigue syndrome
  - Social media post: How to know if you have adrenal fatigue syndrome
  - Infographic: Breaking down the rise of adrenal fatigue syndrome
  - Email newsletter: Do you need a formal diagnosis of adrenal fatigue syndrome?
- Week 2: Blog Post #2, keyword adrenal fatigue causes
  - Social media post: Biggest triggers of adrenal fatigue
  - Email newsletter: What triggered your adrenal fatigue?
  - Lead magnet: 14 causes of adrenal fatigue
- Week 3: Blog Post #3, keyword adrenal fatigue test
  - Lead magnet: Checklist of adrenal fatigue test options
  - Email newsletter: Are all adrenal fatigue tests the same?
  - Social media post: Are adrenal fatigue tests accurate?
- Week 4: Blog Post #4, keyword symptoms of adrenal fatigue
  - Lead magnet: Quiz—Do you have adrenal fatigue?
  - Email newsletter: Which symptoms are most likely signs of adrenal fatigue?

Speaking of editorial calendars, making one is the best way to reduce decision fatigue and create a predictable process for content production. With a calendar, you decide on the topics and publish dates in advance. If you're also the person writing your blogs, this will cut down on decision fatigue because you've already put in the work to define the main topics and keywords.

Keywords should certainly drive your content writing strategy, but don't forget about seasonal details. Here are some examples of how seasonal blog topics might fit into editorial calendars for various businesses:

- A divorce lawyer might know that many filings for divorce happen after the summer and winter holidays. Blogs about how to know if divorce is the right decision for you and what to expect in your first meeting with a lawyer would likely perform well during these times.
- A personal trainer knows that people have a lot of motivation to get things back on track toward the beginning of the year. They might cover topics such as how to stick with resolutions or building healthy habits to coincide with people's natural interest during that time frame.
- A homeowners insurance agency in Florida might target blogs about preparing for hurricane season for posting in early spring.

How to Get into a Blogging Routine

A blogging routine can be developed once you have your editorial calendar in place. When you don't have a calendar, it's easy to spin your wheels for an entire day before you even get started on the post itself. Much like podcasting or regular social media posting, blogging can catch you off guard with the amount of regular work it requires, so you'll want to set yourself up for success as much as possible by doing the prework of keyword selection and topic finalization.

A few things will impact the time commitment for your blogging routine:

- The depth of research required for the topics you've chosen
- Your target word count length
- How often you post
- Whether you're also the same person adding bells and whistles such as pictures after the piece is written
- Your personal writing process

If you're handling the blog writing on your own, plan for at least a few hours per blog post you create. This includes the research, writing, and editing stages. Having worked with many freelance writers, I've found that people are all across the board in terms of the time it takes them to complete a 1,000-word blog. For someone with more experience in the industry and general copywriting knowledge, it might only take a few hours. For a newer writer or someone feeling a lack of confidence with no system in place, it could be much longer. The best thing you can do as a new writer is to feel out what your own process looks like and then look for ways to systematize the work.

Even if you're outsourcing the blog work to another person on your team or to a freelance writer, you'll do some upfront work to make that an organized process. See Chapter 12 for more information about what to do before outsourcing your website content writing process.

The first few weeks of your blogging routine might be carried by momentum. It will get harder after that, but the more you can build a system where you know what to do and when, the easier it will be to stick with your self-imposed deadlines. Here's an example of a possible production schedule if you'll be writing weekly blogs:

- *End of quarter*: Define and confirm all blog topics for the following quarter.
- *End of quarter*: Draft writing guidelines or outlines for month one publish dates.
- *Last two weeks of the quarter*: Draft blog post one for the next quarter.
- *Month one in new quarter*: Edit and publish blog posts, and create outlines for the following month.

How to Create Great Headlines and Titles for Blogs

Your blog's headline is just as important as the subject line you use in an email newsletter. You should put in great effort and research to make sure it lines up with the topic you're discussing and that it captures readers' interest. Crafting an excellent headline is well worth the time. But be aware there is a difference between creating a great headline and clickbait.

Clickbait entices someone with an interesting or controversial title but usually does not deliver on its promise. You don't need buzzworthy headlines. Instead, you need headlines that accurately address your reader's biggest concerns and explain what the entire article will be about. Having a blog is worth nothing if you don't also have a headline that aligns with it. That's how you keep a reader's attention from the moment they land on your website.

You can use tools such as CoSchedule's Headline Analyzer to assess whether you have appropriately incorporated the keyword and developed a thorough headline that will pique readers' interest. Remember to do your keyword research in advance so that you know the primary keyword you're targeting in each blog post.

The CoSchedule Headline Analyzer is an excellent tool to check the score of your primary blog headline. Their algorithm is geared toward list style and how-to titles, and that's because those perform better. There's a free version that you might max out quickly, but it will help you see what kinds of things influence scoring. If you're creating multiple headlines per month, it may be worth paying for this tool, which also has a Chrome extension. It's a handy one to keep with you as you grow your content marketing. You can find this resource at: coschedule.com/headline-analyzer.

I'll give you an example of a headline I ran with the primary keyword "become a freelance writer," something that might be relevant for my own website. When I entered this headline, I scored 52 out of 100. That means I have room for improvement. Tips below the score give me examples of things I could do to improve my score, such as increasing my power words or my word count.

My next move might be to try a title written as a question or as a step-by-step description. By switching over to "how to become a freelance writer," my score actually went down.

In this instance, CoSchedule recommended *uncommon, emotional,* and *power* words to improve my score and the clickthrough rate of my headline. If you don't know what those are, the tool offers examples.

Next, I added in "the ultimate guide" to address the emotional impact suggestion, for a headline of "The ultimate guide: How to become a freelance writer." Doing so increased my score to 72.

Note: In some cases, your "common" words might be a crucial part of your primary keyword, so err on the side of leaving those in. In the example above, CoSchedule flagged *become* as a common word. That makes sense, because it's exactly how someone would search for these results.

Even when you have keywords driving your search engine marketing, you'll want to incorporate your unique voice. Can you add quotes? Is there something specific to your background, such as having been in business for 20 years, that will help make this article a little bit different? Will you use unique subheads and organization of the article? As always, you should never copy what anyone else is doing, either directly or indirectly.

You can look at your competitors to find ways to differentiate what you are doing. Perhaps there's an article that ranks very highly on Google, but it isn't very well-written or the information is outdated. This is an opportunity to create an SEO article with your unique voice in mind, while still getting those SEO benefits.

What to Post: Fitness Trainer Example

Let's walk through an example of what you could potentially post on your blog. Imagine a fitness trainer who intends to promote themselves for personal training sessions. Relevant articles could include fitness tips to help build that trust and knowledge. But people who tend to be into fitness might also be interested in meditation tips; weight loss ideas; breaking down myths about dieting, health, and fitness; nutritious eating; quick and easy meal planning; reviews of CrossFit; or new types of exercise or exercise videos that have come out recently. Or they might want to read about general exercise guidance, such as common mistakes people make in the gym or with weights, medical benefits of exercise and how that can translate to other areas of life, or how you can hurt yourself if you don't know what you're doing. Or perhaps this trainer could write a series of articles about exercising too long, exercising too often, using too much weight, or doing too much cardio and not enough strength training.

All these articles target SEO keywords while also building the credibility of the fitness trainer, because they have the opportunity to talk about their unique perspective and convince readers they really know what they're doing. And then they might add new stories about current research around fitness benefits, weight loss, or even how many people are not exercising. That could be a great way to capitalize on something that's already trending.

Whether I'm writing for myself or for a client, I usually start with a brain dump and brainstorm all the different categories we could use. In this trainer example, we might have fitness tips, healthy living tips, healthy eating, meal planning, and even meditation. And that makes it really easy to provide enough variety for the reader without going too far in the direction of losing some of that SEO traction.

Talking to More Than One Reader

Your primary readership likely includes more than one target audience.

Let's look at an example. My primary purpose is to help freelancers and online business owners scale their company in less time and with fewer headaches, and ultimately make them more money in the process. My blog categories include outsourcing, general business tips, freelance marketing, productivity, freelance writing, Upwork, and working as a virtual assistant. It's important to remember that my audience might shift from one blog post to the next. Our personal trainer from the previous example might have one reader who's a marathon runner who is not at all interested in strength training, but they could also have readers who are interested in all the content they post.

My potential audience typically includes stay-at-home parents, millennials, retirees looking for something to do now that they've loved and left their primary job, business owners stuck around the $5,000- to $8,000-a-month income level who are looking to grow, and business owners who feel burned out or overwhelmed. And then I've also found I have a niche audience with teachers and journalists who are looking for a side hustle or career change.

Trying to reach everyone would mean my SEO would have sort of a diluted effect. I want to keep my potential audience in the back of my mind, because that helps me infuse the types of keywords those readers are looking for. Something that I write specifically for retirees will look completely different from what I write for Millennials. At the same time, a blog article about places to find clients online could be equally relevant for both. So when you're creating an SEO article or blog, keep that in mind. Will this be specific to a particular group? Or does this apply to multiple sections of your audience?

Linking Basics

On your own site, you'll want to link to both other relevant pages on your website and to other credible websites. A link to another high-quality website can help back up claims you make and should be used every time you reference a statistic or a specific quote. This is good SEO practice overall.

If you wish to have a call to action in an individual blog post, put it at the end. Perhaps you want your readers to sign up for your email newsletter, so you can send them updates on your blog and other content marketing. Don't do this multiple times throughout your post or put it at the beginning, because when readers who are only there for information discover you are promoting yourself, you'll lose them.

Understanding Do Follow vs. Nofollow Links

Within the world of linking are two primary categories: do follow, or follow links, and nofollow links. If you are in the outreach process to gain backlinks to your website, you might assume these are one and the same. After all, they both link to anchor text on someone else's website to drive traffic back to your own. But nofollow links and do follow links are different. A nofollow tag is a way to tell a search engine that the link essentially doesn't count. Nofollow links are added by including REL='no follow' in the html of your links. The main purpose for using nofollow links is to cut down on search engine spam. For instance, links in certain types of content, such as blog post comments or social media, tend to default to nofollow. That makes it harder for spammers who post their links there to rank in Google searches. Do follow links, however, carry SEO benefits and can improve your website ranking and your overall credibility.

The more do follow links you earn from other websites, the better. The easiest links to get, however, are nofollow links, and do follow links can be much harder to get for someone who is relatively new. Another thing to be mindful of when asking for links on other websites is how many other sites they link to on that same page. The type of link and the page itself will influence the quality of the link benefits, meaning if the person publishing

CONTENT IS KING

your website link has also named 20 other companies on that same page, the relative impact for your website link is greatly reduced. Spammy pages that overuse a quantity strategy are more likely to perform poorly.

Once a link has been added to a website, its impact will usually last for as long as it stays on the site. If something happens to the site, the page is deleted, or the link is purposely removed, then the link will be gone for good.

Chapter 9 Action Steps & Takeaways

- Decide: Does blogging fit into your core content marketing strategy?
- Create an editorial calendar, if applicable.
- Determine how you'll build internal or external links into your blogs.

CHAPTER 10

Advanced Blogging

Now that you know some of the benefits of blogging, it's time to think about the specifics of how to build it into your overall strategy. Once you've created a cadence for determining and writing content, you want to make sure each piece you post on your blog includes all the important copywriting and SEO elements. In this chapter, you'll learn more about advanced blogging techniques, including how to build an idea bank, how to think like a reader, how to use categories and tags, how to repurpose content, and how to use analytics.

Building Core and Additional Content on Your Blog

Once you've covered some of the basics on your blog, such as questions you're frequently asked, where do you go from there?

CONTENT IS KING

Your core content will be the topics of most interest to your audience, based on their needs. As mentioned earlier, you'll want to go a little deeper into specifics with your holistic content marketing strategy, but you also need to cover some of the basics. I like to call the basics "circles of content." These are the pieces and general topics every blog should have, based on its own keyword research.

Coming up with ideas for additional content, though, is a challenge for many new business owners. I strongly recommend that you build your own system for capturing ideas so you can review them in the future. This is true whether you plan to keep the writing in-house or outsource it to a writer.

I do a lot of writing about car accidents and personal injury claims. Because of that, I've really refined a system to capture my ideas. That means I have a massive idea bank to pull from, if I'm not finding any inspiration.

Core Content

The most obvious content is the easiest to access. For a weight loss blog managed by a nutritionist or personal trainer, you might be thinking of exercises or recipes you could suggest to your clients, or your favorite weight loss tips. These are the core pieces of content that speak most specifically to the target audience.

Your primary circles of content should be the topics that are most relevant and accessible to your readers. This content is directly relevant to the SEO tags and keywords that are most important for website-ranking purposes. Of course, because this content is somewhat generic, other people will target the same keywords. Ultimately, the goal is to base the foundation of your website content on long-tail keywords and supplement that content with short-tail keywords. Generic content on its own (or specific content on its own) is unlikely to help the website rank.

Let's imagine an example related to weight loss. If your website primarily targets people who are looking to lose weight, your gut reaction might be that everything you write about needs to be associated with diet, perhaps supplemented by content related to workout plans. However, these are only the most basic concepts in that topic area, and your readers likely have other interests as well. Furthermore, because such stiff competition exists for weight loss blogs on the internet, you'll need to create materials in a way that is specific to you and your company, which you can ultimately link to those core pages.

What Else Do Your Readers Care About?

One level beyond the most basic and obvious level of content includes things that might also be relevant to that same audience but maybe aren't weight-loss specific. People who care about weight loss will also be interested in related subjects that might expand well beyond typical diet, weight loss, and recipe topics. So your target reader might be going back to the gym or starting a running regimen. And a related concern could be:

> *Do I need special shoes to do that? What shoes do I buy if I haven't worked out in 10 years and I'm going to the shoe store to pick something up? Do I get cross trainers? Do I get walking shoes? Do I get running shoes?*

Maybe you write about how to get your shoes fitted properly. Another fun idea could be apps to help you find a friend to exercise with who will keep you motivated. And you could provide some stats in there about how having some form of accountability helps people achieve their workout goals.

Some people choose to pursue weight loss without doing any exercise at all. So that exercise focus might not be relevant to the entire audience of the weight loss blog, but it is related content outside that simple core. You could also talk about other things in the health and wellness space. So you might be researching the connection between diet, sleep, and weight. How are all these topics tied together? What role does stress have in helping someone feel motivated when waking up in the morning? That might not initially seem relevant for a weight loss blog, but it is. A person who wakes up in a bad mood or feeling tired is not going to the gym. They will have a harder time doing their meal prep, and they're planning for different things.

Remember Your Target Audience

Remember from Chapter 3 the work you did to define your target audience. Who is this person who we hope will read the blog? How did they spend their day? Are they in a particular age category? Are we trying to reach a particular gender? Are we trying to reach someone who has a very specific problem? Considering those questions is a great way to expand beyond that basic idea of content. It's almost like creating a character for a fiction book. Who is this person? What motivates them? What challenges do they face in their life? What is leading them to search for this particular issue? Why are they taking that specific action? What other content might be relevant for that specific person as they're reading through this information?

Max Out Your Content Ideas

Your own brain is the inspiration for this initial list of possible content ideas. But you certainly don't need to stop there. Sources of additional ideas for your blog are everywhere.

Once you have maxed out everything you can think of for initial content, supplement your list by researching and identifying other possibilities for topics and titles. Use this as an opportunity to collect as much information as possible, and don't worry about editing your list until you have gone through each of the following sources and come up with as much material as possible. This is how you can build your master brain dump list.

Authoritative Organizations

Think about who the influencers and major changemakers are in your industry. You don't necessarily need to link to competitor content, but you can still capitalize on all the SEO benefits of linking to high-quality websites that produce research and materials relevant to your target audience. Perhaps, for example, you are a caregiver to an elderly loved one. You might choose to blog about the impacts of Alzheimer's disease and keep your blog updated with material about the latest studies and research for Alzheimer's patients. Of course, you will provide credit where credit is due and link to the proper websites when you do this, but you will also be building on the fact that you are showing knowledge and awareness in the space. It is much easier to present your website as a resource hub for your clients when you are already doing the work behind the scenes to present them with relevant and timely material.

Google Alerts

One easy way to max out possible content ideas is to follow relevant resources online. As a personal injury law blog writer, I set Google Alerts to receive updates from the National Highway Traffic Safety Administration, the Centers for Disease Control, and the AAA Foundation. This ensures that relevant content arrives in my inbox on a regular basis. When I'm looking for inspiration for something timely and relevant, I can find it and link directly to high-quality sources that will ultimately help the blog perform more effectively.

Come up with a list of relevant tags you can use to set up Google Alerts. For example, if you're a dentist looking for new blog title ideas, you might set up Google Alerts for:

- Dentistry study
- Flossing study
- Oral disease

YouTube

You can also get great ideas for blog content by looking at YouTube. Search engine tools function similarly on other websites as well. For example, most people are aware of the connection between YouTube and Google (Google owns YouTube), but it's easy to forget that YouTube is actually a search engine in and of itself. People use it every day to search for content. For this reason, you might head over to YouTube and see what kinds of questions and topics people are searching for. YouTube makes this easy. When you start typing a series of words into the search bar, YouTube will attempt to populate what the algorithm expects you to look for. This tells you more about what other people are seeking out on this search engine.

Thinking Like Your Audience

One of the most powerful ways to directly address the needs of your primary readers is to think about the kinds of questions they ask. What questions have clients asked you in the past? What are people asking your sales team? This method helps you craft content specifically for your target audience. Your readers will feel as though you can solve their specific concerns.

One of my freelance writing clients shared that some of his customers were concerned about whether filing married taxes separately or jointly influenced student loan repayment options. We did the keyword research to phrase this concern as a question in the blog title. This had multiple benefits. First of all, the client already knew this was a hot topic and one he had personally worked through with clients. And he was able, from this blog post, to direct them to book consultations with him because he showcased that he was an expert, but each situation was different and would require a consultation. This signals to readers that the accountant has already handled this kind of complex case.

Second, this post provided information in the form of a question and answer for the end readers of the article, who would likely start by typing that question into search engines. Using the same question increases the chances that the audience will click on the article and read the whole thing.

If you don't have actual client data to pull from, you can still think about the state of mind of your readers when they click on the search engine. Let's imagine that the blog in question belongs to a financial professional. I might start brainstorming by thinking about questions that would ultimately lead someone to a financial professional. What would prompt somebody to call a financial professional? Perhaps they've had a major windfall and don't know what to do with it. Maybe they just turned 35 or 40 and realize they haven't done enough or anything for retirement planning and are ready to get serious. Maybe they've inherited some type of stock or large asset and aren't sure about the best way to leverage this over the course of their future. Maybe they recently completed a debt consolidation program or read a book about financial planning and are looking for the next steps to implement this into their life.

All these scenarios provide clues to the mindset of the person who might end up on the financial professional's blog. We might even create content that targets each of the people in these situations. This helps to draw the connection between the reader and the website while also drawing in SEO. When you can balance those keywords and other technical aspects of SEO with the psychological perspective of the person who is searching at that point in time, you can build that know, like, and trust factor with your reader.

From here, you will likely have tons of ideas you can write about, which supplement the keyword research you did earlier. I like to store all this information in a document or a spreadsheet. If you include the metrics that are most important to you, such as number of keyword searches per month or the relevance each idea has for your audience, you can sort by those metrics later. You can return to this database or brain bank when you need inspiration as you build your quarterly or monthly editorial calendar.

Organizing and Planning

The next phase of building your content marketing calendar is to organize all the ideas you have collected. Some will ultimately be turned into blog posts or other pieces of content marketing, such as infographics or social media posts. One key aspect of this is to determine the right title. When planning blog titles, make sure the primary keyword is included, but also that the blog title accurately describes the material that will follow in the blog post itself.

The blog should also flow from the beginning to the end, providing helpful information for the reader in a sensible way. Imagine the following example, where you've determined you want your blog title to be "Is power washing safe for pets?"

What might the reader's experience be if the order of the blog with that title was as follows?

- Where to buy power-washing tools
- Chemicals in power washing
- How to power wash
- How often to power wash

This would be a confusing experience for the reader, right? First of all, only the second subhead addresses the primary purpose of their search (and your post title). Someone who is trying to find out whether power washing is safe is probably curious about whether it is safe with different types of machines and whether it is better to do it by yourself or outsource to a professional. Having only one section of this blog directly addressing the chemicals included in the power-washing process could be confusing.

Furthermore, starting the blog with where to buy power-washing tools doesn't really match the intent or create the ideal flow. Putting that information at the end of the block, after you have made a compelling argument about whether power washing is safe, would make a lot more sense. Make sure the content flows in an order that will be logical to a reader. You might come back to this a couple of times before beginning to draft a blog, but that's OK. It is well worth the effort to make sure you actually meet your reader where they are.

A better outline for this topic might be:

- Is power washing safe around pets?
- Chemicals used in power washing
- How to power wash safely

Generic vs. Specific

By now you know that some questions and topics that pop up in your keyword research may seem very general in nature. When coming up with topics for your blog, strike a balance between things that are more specific (usually your long-tail keywords) and those more general topics, so your site becomes a resource hub.

Here's what I mean by generic content: It's something that 15 to 20 other people have already written about in depth. Because Google ranking competition is so fierce, it will be really hard for a generic topic to rank if that's all you have on your site.

And because prospective readers have so many choices, they have no reason to select that particular blog to read. We don't want to try to compete with everyone on generic content. The internet is flooded with millions of new pages every single day. Your content must stand out, and one way to do that is to do a deeper dive. So let's talk about why the following three sample blog topics are not necessarily a great choice:

- How to fix a flat tire
- How to check your car's oil on your own
- When to get car maintenance

These topics would definitely be relevant for a car mechanic who's trying to run a blog. However, if we post the blog on how to fix a flat tire, that mechanic is competing with everyone around the world who has a blog post called "How to fix a flat tire." There's no differentiation, so it probably won't attract the exact readership that mechanic wants. But if that mechanic is in Pittsburgh, Pennsylvania, and only services clients in the Pittsburgh region, we could make that title or topic specific to Pittsburgh, such as "Places in Pittsburgh you're most likely to get a flat tire" or "What to do if you get a flat tire on X Street in Pittsburgh."

Another way to differentiate it might be to write about how to fix a flat tire when you have no tools in your car. Are there any ways to temporarily fix a flat until you can get to a mechanic or call for help? If you can help people who have none of the tools and no spare in their car, that's something they might want to read. Although the generic content of how to fix a flat tire is probably super helpful, we need to add some type of twist beyond that generic content. If this blog is helpful to readers, it might help the mechanic's site to rank in a search for "how to fix a flat tire" for searchers all over the country. A local mechanic, however, just wants clients in their specific region.

Remember SEO

Remember, we want to design content for SEO, answering those key questions and concerns a prospective client would have for you. Let's say you're a relationship coach, writing a blog on how to recover after a breakup. You're probably thinking that's a good place to start. But we need something more tailored than that, because there's a lot of material out there on that topic. So you need a unique spin that infuses the tone and voice of you, the relationship coach, in a way that draws an ideal client.

A good example might be "10 exercises that help after a breakup" or something else specific to your process. In this case, think about the process you as the coach would use to help someone jump back into the dating pool after a long time out of it.

If your ideal audience is women in their 30s who are looking to settle down, we want to take that generic title example and tailor it to who those women want to speak to. Your content has dual purposes. It's not just about ranking in the search engines. It's about communicating clearly on topics your reader cares about.

How to Think Like a Reader

You want to strike a balance in your blog content, where you're providing helpful information to the reader and also sending all the right signals to the search engines.

Before you even come up with ideas, the most important thing you can do is think like a reader. You yourself are the Googler. In fact, when I started my freelance writing journey, I literally Googled "how to become a freelance writer" and kind of fell down the rabbit hole, reading things. So when you come up with ideas and blog titles, think like a reader.

We are saturated with information lately. Information comes at you through your email inbox, your social media feed, advertisements, TV, and streaming devices. You have an endless flow of information. But think about what you do when you have a question or a concern, or when you're looking for a very specific type of person. How do you approach the search process? You type it into Google, right? If I've moved to a new area and I need a haircut, what happens if I type "hairstylist" into Google? That will probably give me a bunch of pages about what it pays to be a hairstylist and what training you need to become a hairstylist, best rated hairstylist in Chicago, best hairstylist for curly hair. So think about that search process. As you're coming up with topics, consider your clients' main concerns, issues, and questions that lead them to Google and how they find information about a specific problem.

What would get your client's attention? What would prompt someone to open and read the article you posted? SEO content needs to go one step beyond providing helpful information that is aligned with where the reader is in the funnel. Your content also needs to capture your reader's attention, usually with a meaningful topic and an excellent headline and title.

Using Categories and Tags

Categories and tags are tools you can use to organize your blog content as it grows. They make it easier for readers to find the most relevant content for them. Quick definitions of these tools are as follows:

- Categories: Broad topics
- Tags: Smaller topics

If you are a business coach who focuses mostly on time management and productivity, those two concepts might be the main categories on your blog. You might also use tags such as "software" or "delegating" to help readers sort through all your past material. Having a good category structure when you start makes it easier to scale.

Videocasting, Podcasting, and Blogging: How to Repurpose Content

One alternative to creating a blog strategy from scratch is to repurpose audio recordings from a podcast. For this to work, you've got to be a little more creative than copying and pasting the audio transcript onto your website (although there are benefits to providing that transcript as a downloadable PDF option for accessibility purposes).

If you run a regular podcast, you know a lot of work goes into creating and producing it. You should have a strategy that gives you the most mileage for every single episode.

You can repurpose your existing video or audio into written formats. For example, I have repurposed my 10- to 15-minute Facebook Live videos into text-based-quote social shares, image-based social shares, one-minute video clips, and even full blogs. The main idea here is to keep the essence of your main points and teachings while cleaning up the text so it reads well in written form. When we talk, we frequently say things like "um," "you know," and "so." Any transcripts will have to be cleaned up before you publish.

Here are a few tools that can help you with the repurposing process:

- Descript or Otter.ai can create automated transcripts of your video or audio files quickly.
- Grammarly can help you find major errors from spoken to written word in an uploaded document. (Their Chrome extension also makes grammar checking simple in Google Docs.)
- Headliner.app (and others) let you upload audio files to turn them into short video clips.

When looking for material for social media posts, create templates inside a tool like Canva to make sure the branding is consistent. You can pull main ideas, quotes from a guest or host, or the title of the episode into social media image templates that you use each time you release an episode. If you've got an in-house graphic designer, they can make new designs for each episode. If you're looking to keep costs down, pay a graphic designer once to make you a full suite of templates that you can add new headshots and text to every week.

Understanding Bounce Rate

Most of the purpose of creating SEO-rich content is to ensure that people get to your website and stay on it. After all, if a reader leaves your site relatively quickly, that signals to search engines that the content the reader landed on is not relevant or helpful to them. That information is captured in a metric known as bounce rate. The term refers to the number of people who leave your website after visiting only one page.

This is why the design of the home page as well as the rest of your website is so important for presenting a good user experience the first time someone interacts with your brand. If you want to lower your bounce rate, your visitors must see a minimum of two pages on your site every time they visit. Creating relevant links between your own website (inbound links) is an excellent way to draw this connection and to play within SEO guidelines appropriately. You can also use navigational or menu tools to present alternative links throughout your website. For example, a child custody lawyer with a blog post on "joint vs. full custody" might link to their own services page on child custody within that blog. That's an inbound link.

Do not exclude links to other websites, as these are also a cornerstone of your SEO strategy. But be sure to supplement them with high-quality inbound links to relevant information. Be careful about providing too many opportunities for a person to click away from your site or making it difficult for them to navigate your site. A great example of this is advertisements or pop-ups. When pop-ups take up too much of the site, especially on mobile devices or when they are annoying, a visitor is much more likely to leave after visiting one page, thus increasing your bounce rate. Using plug-ins or software tools that help create pop-ups and ads can tell you more about how well the quantity and timing of pop-ups and ads are working.

Using Analytics to Improve Content

It is a lot of work to get all your content marketing up and listed. However, you cannot ignore the possibility of needing to come back and audit this material as you go. Some blog topics might have made sense at the moment but perform poorly over time. Having a regular content audit process in place will make it easier for you to not only update material and keep it as relevant as possible, but also remove material that is no longer helpful or is performing poorly.

A tool called Hotjar uses heat maps to tell you how people access your website and how long they spend on certain parts of the site. You can also see where people hovered before clicking, and all this information can be used to improve your content as well as the overall design.

Heat maps are a great tool to see how people use your website in real time. You'll build your site with the best intentions for user navigation, but you might need to make changes based on how people use your site. You might discover with heat mapping, for example, that 90 percent of users don't scroll past the top third of your website page. If you've got important info below that, you'll need to rearrange the page structure or find another way to convey that information.

Chapter 10 Action Steps & Takeaways

- ✈ Define your core content.
- ✈ Make a giant list of content ideas.
- ✈ Organize and plan your content calendar.
- ✈ Decide if you'll repurpose content and how.

CHAPTER 11

Marketing Outreach: Other Content

Services pages and blogs are not your only options for connecting with readers and encouraging them to take the next action step. You might use a few other kinds of pages on your website in a more fluid way than the rest of your website content. Not every business will need them, but it's good to understand their use cases and how to get the most out of them. In this chapter, we'll explore sales pages, landing pages, lead magnets, and case studies.

While much of your site will be information-focused, sales and landing pages are driven by a call to action. The main goal of these pages is to drive your reader to take the next action with you.

A sales page drives someone to buy something, while a landing page usually encourages them to take a nonpurchase action, such as scheduling a free consultation call or downloading a report.

Landing and sales pages are great opportunities to generate immediate interest from a website visitor, but to achieve success, they must inspire prompt action.

Sales Copy

Sales copy is just what it sounds like: website content designed to get someone to buy. This can be anything from a $5 offer all the way up to investments of thousands. From physical products to service offerings to books and online courses, sales copy is designed to make a reader feel the pain of their current problem and see that your offering is a solution. Make no bones about it: Sales copy is a completely different style of writing than website content writing or writing for SEO. Sales copy is an art form that takes many copywriters years to learn. If you're not familiar with sales copy but see a need for it, this is one opportunity to outsource the work to a professional writer.

Sales copy does a lot of the heavy lifting in your business, so you can't afford to make mistakes here or take your best guess. Many factors go into selling a product or service, but bad copy hinders too many business owners from achieving the conversion rates they desire. It's often the first thing to look at when a marketing funnel isn't performing as planned, and it's also one area where making some minor changes can fuel big results.

Elements of Great Sales Copy

While the length and overall style of sales copy might change from one company to another, a couple of core threads should be in place throughout. They include:

- A focus more on the benefits of an offer than its features
- Emotional triggers that make the reader feel as though you're speaking directly to them

How to Understand Benefits vs. Features

One big mistake made in the realm of sales copy is listing out all the features of an offer instead of the benefits. Both elements belong in your sales copy, but if you had to choose one that's more important, it's the benefits.

One of these refers to tangible aspects of your offer and the other refers to intangible aspects. Features are tangible—those are the direct things customers will receive by purchasing. For example, if you are a life coach, the tangible features you offer to clients are the weekly sessions that you would coach with them. Benefits, however, are what those features can do for them.

In the life coach example, the benefits of engaging in life coaching are feeling more confident, owning your productivity, and setting and achieving goals you can be proud of. The vast majority of sales copy should address benefits.

Benefits—what you are truly selling—are based on emotions, while features are what you think you are selling. When people purchase a product or a service from you, they are not only purchasing that product; they are purchasing the transformation or the outcome they'll get from that product. Focusing too much of your sales copy on the factual features of what someone will get decreases the chance of conversion.

Let's dive into the concept of benefits and features with an example of a pressure cooker. Pressure cookers have surged in popularity in recent years. Many of them come with plenty of features, which might be the buttons that allow someone to set the time for cooking and to cook a variety of sweet and savory options. However, a benefit of using the pressure cooker is it speeds up cooking time and allows people to get dinner on their table faster. You can tell which is more compelling for a potential buyer. The buyer is truly making their purchase for what it can enable in their life, which in this case means faster, delicious dinners on the table. The features are just something that supports the overall benefit the person is receiving.

How to Leverage Emotion in Sales Copy

One way to improve your connection with your audience and encourage them to act is through the power of emotions. One of the most compelling emotional motivations is time. All too often, advertisers and copywriters focus on making life simpler or saving money, and these are certainly compelling benefits for someone using a service or a product. But saving time is increasingly important. People are more overloaded than ever with responsibilities and feeling stressed from their jobs. Time is something you can't get more of and yet is profoundly important.

If time (or lack of it) is a trigger for your audience, you might infuse that concept into your sales copy.

Another way to introduce time-based emotions throughout your sales copy is to consider the instant gratification society we live in. Words like *right now*, *immediately*, and *instantly* all speak to people who want their solution faster.

As the global COVID-19 pandemic showed us, time is precious and people are choosing to value it more and more. Using time as a sales copy technique can include telling someone they can save time doing something they don't want to do, encouraging them to stop wasting valuable time with a process that could be automated or simplified, or helping them spend more quality time on activities they do want to do.

Luxury and Influence

The desire for luxury and influence is another emotional trigger you can use if those desires embody your ideal audience member. This taps into the idea of prestige, which can make you feel good or make others see you and your business in a particular way. Elements such as exclusivity, which can align with luxury or influence, can also help you stand out in the market.

Family

For most people, belonging to a family, whether found or biological, is an important component of their life. The more you can play up the concept of family, the easier it will be to forge connections with your audience's ideals. For example, think about advertisements that talk about keeping the family together, keeping them healthy, allowing children to enjoy their childhood, how their family may struggle without their financial contributions, and more.

Here are some examples:

- If you're writing about life insurance, talk about providing a legacy for the audience's family.
- If you're writing about vacations, talk about the importance of making memories with family.

➤ If you're providing parenting tips, tap into the fact that a parent searching for advice wants to do their best but might feel inadequate.

Landing Pages and Lead Magnets

What happens if someone lands on your website, gets value from what you've posted, but then disappears only to forget about you and your company name? To avoid this, most companies include a landing page and lead magnet strategy in their business. This gives the company permission to remarket to that same follower multiple times. When someone fills out a landing page, they're usually sharing an email address or a phone number. For sharing that information, the reader receives some kind of free offering.

You might hear the terms *ethical bribe*, *opt in*, *freebie*, or *lead magnet* used to describe the free offering you give to someone in exchange for them joining your email list, social media group, or text message marketing. These all essentially mean the same thing, which is that you're creating and giving away something free to introduce the reader to your expertise. This is a strongly recommended part of your marketing funnel. Once people know the quality of your free information, they will likely feel more confident investing in your paid materials.

Landing Page Basics

A landing page can receive traffic from pop-ups, ads, social media posts, or links in your email newsletter, among other places.

The landing page is the place where you offer your lead magnet, a free item such as a report, checklist, video series, or audio file. The landing page can be as simple as a few lines of text with an image of what is being offered, along with a place where they can add sign-up details such as their name and email address. It can also be much more involved if you're trying to get them to commit to something more complicated, such as a five-day challenge.

On a landing page, the primary goal is to get the reader to realize there is a significant benefit for signing up for the offer. This means you need to make it compelling and directly aligned with their primary pain point. Once your landing page is live, you will measure its success based on the conversion rate. The conversion rate is the number of people who have viewed the page compared with the number of people who have signed up for that particular offer. When evaluating a landing page that is performing poorly, you might look at the copy, the images, the detail or level of information requested from the subscriber, or the offer itself.

Lead Magnet Basics

Your lead magnet might be an ebook, a PDF, a checklist, or a quiz. These are tools to encourage people to join your email list. As part of your bigger content marketing strategy, the primary purpose here is to provide information that goes beyond the basics or to give people a usable template or checklist.

Here are some examples of how various companies might use lead magnets:

- A personal trainer might create a PDF of their favorite healthy smoothie recipes.
- A landscaping company could create a checklist of top end-of-summer tasks that anyone can do to improve the health of their lawn before winter hits.
- A company culture specialist might create an assessment or a quiz that companies can use to score themselves on how great their workplace is.

Lead magnets highlight expertise and take the reader one step further in the marketing funnel.

A lead magnet is directly connected to the landing page, because the two work together. The landing page sells the benefit of the lead magnet, but the lead magnet is where you deliver on your promise.

A few other ideas you might consider as a lead magnet include the following:

- A quiz that gives someone a very specific result

- A checklist that helps readers ensure they've considered all the details or steps of a process
- A free report that debunks a myth or simplifies a process
- Swipe files or templates that make it easier for the reader to do something

Sometimes content creators or business owners go overboard with their lead magnet. After all, if giving a one-page PDF helps highlight value, wouldn't it be better to offer a 15-page PDF? In most cases, the answer is no.

One of the biggest challenges marketers and customers face right now is overwhelm. From spending too much time on video to having too many emails to being targeted with too many advertisements, customers are savvier than ever, but they are also overloaded with messages. The more you can make your lead magnet easy or simple for someone to take on, the easier it will be for them to absorb it and to feel an immediate win. Providing too much information can make the reader feel like the process is too difficult, and they'll walk away feeling that you're knowledgeable but that they are not ready to continue with the project.

For example, imagine that you're a closet organization specialist. You might offer a lead magnet that gives someone a 15-step process to reorganize every closet in their home. Your intention is well-meaning, but a person who is buried in clutter will simply find this overwhelming. You might start with a smaller piece of the process, such as how to set goals for picking things to give away to charity or for a garage sale. This is only one step of the process, but it can give someone an easy, early win that makes them feel motivated to continue with the process and believe that you're the right person to help them. Small, bite-size achievements and wins are best to target here, so continue to edit your work down again and again until you feel you have given someone a quick, clear, achievable outcome.

Tips for Writing Lead Magnets

If you plan to create lead magnets, here are a few important notes to keep in mind.

CONTENT IS KING

Tip 1: Know Your Customer

The first rule of writing lead magnets is to know the customer. Who is the end reader who will be enticed by this particular freebie? Lean into their pain points. Think carefully as you brainstorm ideas for possible lead magnets. What are the biggest challenges they face in their daily life? What obstacles are they most interested in overcoming? What keeps them up at night?

A great way to find this information is to search questions on Reddit, AnswerThePublic, or Amazon reviews. You'll get a lot of amazing information about what's important to people, such as what drove them crazy about a product or what they loved about a particular service. Exploring these sites is also a great way to pull keywords. What is most important to your potential clients? Let's say you are a podcast production company and you're trying to reach somebody who wants to launch a podcast. You might go through AnswerThePublic and look for phrases such as "how hard is it to start a podcast?" to see what actual people have said about it.

The purpose here is not to steal work that others have already done. Instead, you're finding an insight into where others have not gone far enough to answer questions and how you might be able to position your lead magnet as the answer to a common concern. You will learn a lot more about the pain points of your ideal audience.

Tip 2: Match Your Magnet

The next thing to consider is creating a lead magnet that matches where your audience is in the funnel. Remember the person who's getting ready to make that podcast? We don't want to offer them something at the awareness level. If they're making decisions such as "Where should I host my podcast?" or "How should I create the show art for my podcast?" we don't want to give them "Five Steps to Launching Your Podcast" or "Three Tech Tools for Creating a Podcast." They're already past that point. And likewise, we don't want to offer something that's really far down the funnel for someone who's only at the awareness stage, because they're not ready to make a commitment yet. It doesn't help them.

Tip 3: Don't Overwhelm Your Customer

A common mistake in lead magnets is giving too much. Many companies do this with the best of intentions. They think, well, if giving something away for free is a great model to build trust, what if I give away something extremely valuable for free? This often backfires, because too much information is simply overwhelming. I've seen, time and time again, that these overwhelming lead magnets do not convert as well. Instead, try to pick something concise.

I used to have a 20-page report on Upwork, and people just didn't buy it until I switched it to a one-page profile checklist. That thing converted like gangbusters. I am continually looking at ideas and testing them as lead magnets, and I encourage you to do the same.

A good portion of information for people to consume is a three-step offer, such as "Three Steps to Choosing Your Business's Domain Name." This doesn't promise them everything they need to know about starting a business, but it gives them one particular piece, which is clarity on how to choose a domain name.

What wouldn't work, on the other hand, is something like "67 Steps to Starting Your First Website." That might seem like a really good giveaway, because you've organized all 67 steps, right? You've told the reader everything they need to know. But it will be really overwhelming for people. And they'll probably get stuck on step two and not do any of the rest. So break it down. Maybe some of those 67 steps can be put into an email sequence. And some could go into a paid ebook or a course at the end of the funnel. But we don't want to throw everything at people at once.

Tip 4: Avoid an Unclear Outcome

A lead magnet description that is too vague or otherwise not clear can cause a disconnect with a reader. If people don't understand what they're getting, they will not opt in for your "Hear More about My Thoughts on This" or to "Join My Weekly Newsletter," even if those thoughts or newsletter are free.

A good example might be "Six Steps to Filing Your Taxes in Two Hours or Less." As a potential customer, I'm like *Yeah, I do not want to spend more than two hours working on my taxes this year.* What is less great here is this lead magnet copy doesn't tell me anything about what's in the report. It doesn't tell me if this addresses taxes for business or if it's specific to a certain state. As a potential customer, I'm wondering if this is just a promotional report selling an accountant's services. Make sure your lead magnet description is really specific and clear, because I promise you that people will not opt in for a vague offer.

Tip 5: Avoid Bad Design

The design of your lead magnet does need to look professional. Bad design of a lead magnet can shortchange your results or kill amazing content.

A professional design can include your color branding, or it can be in templates you've created. It shouldn't just be something you throw together in Microsoft Word. When it comes to design, don't just export a Word document into a PDF and give that away. Put copyright language on it. Include the company's name and website. We want it to be branded. Once a reader has learned something from your lead magnet, they want to easily be able to contact you for work.

How to Align a Lead Magnet with Your Target Customer

We've talked about lead magnets at a very high level. Now let's dive into how to align a lead magnet with where the customer is in the marketing funnel. You need to know the customer's awareness status and where they are in that process. You always want to meet the reader exactly where they are. If they're at the top of the funnel and not even aware there's a problem yet, much less a solution, you don't want to give them a side-by-side comparison of your company's offer against that of your competitors.

Your awareness-stage reader is not quite ready to make that level of decision yet. Instead, our goal is to build trust and move these readers further along the funnel. The lead magnet, no matter what it is, should always provide a quick win. It shouldn't be so overwhelming that the person feels like they can't accomplish it, or that they don't even finish reading or working through it. Your lead magnet should give them a quick win, both in the sense of how long it takes for them to consume but also in the specificity of the offer itself.

You don't want to tell your audience how to solve all 12 problems they have. Instead, narrow in on one. Then because they were able to establish one quick win from the free material, they will be curious to hang around and see what else is out there. You've built some trust. When a reader is at the awareness stage, a few types of lead magnets make the most sense for them. These include blog posts, white papers, webinars, tools, and audio files such as meditations or affirmations.

Free trials, on the other hand, give someone who's already in the buying stage an opportunity to decide if they like the company. In exchange for sharing their email address and setting up an account, they get to see if the product or service works for them before making a bigger commitment. Free short sessions can work really well for consultants, coaches, and practitioners of things like astrology or anything like that. In this instance, those business owners are delivering a service, a short consultation, a discovery call, or perhaps a sample session. These all provide the opportunity to decide if someone is the right fit. And I find that these short calls can be really powerful when you know that your reader or customer is in the decision phase.

Case Studies

Feedback from people who have worked with you is really powerful for storytelling with new readers on your site. Case studies are very strong social proof stories about someone's experience working with you. Case studies might exist as their own individual blog updates or pages on your website, as lead magnets, or as email newsletter topics. If you want to resonate with your followers, you might use case studies to tell a story about what your past clients experienced.

Gathering this information is slightly different from creating a blog post from scratch. However, you can use case studies in many ways. Case studies help connect people with the role you play as the expert guide in the customer hero's journey. You might want to capitalize on someone who showed interest by getting them to take one action step beyond visiting your website, so you could provide a case study as a lead magnet for becoming an email subscriber. That gives you further permission to contact that reader by coming into their email inbox with the other content you've created to drive them back to your website or to take additional steps with your company, such as scheduling a phone call to learn more about your services. The choice is up to you and depends on where you're targeting customers in the marketing funnel.

Why Are Case Studies Important?

As we've discussed in this chapter, people don't buy features; they buy benefits. They're buying the possibility of the transformation they might achieve by working with you or using your product.

The purpose of a case study is to tell the journey of the transformation another client bought from you. For example, you likely picked up this book because you wanted to feel more confident in your website copywriting process. You didn't buy the book because it had a certain number of pages or a certain number of chapters.

Case studies are extremely effective for conversions. The person in the case study isn't just a happy customer. Instead, this customer went one step further by sharing their story. Their words will resonate with readers because readers will connect with that customer's pain points. Case studies are a great marketing tool to have in your arsenal, because you can repurpose them in many formats beyond your website.

Here are some tips on how to use case studies more effectively:

- Focus on the pain points the customer had before they used your product or service. This helps to clearly showcase the "before" picture, so the transformation is more obvious later.
- Showcase what the customer experienced during the process. (Hint: This is part of your UVP! Refer back to Chapter 3 for more info.)
- End the case study with what the customer experienced at the end of the transformation. What did they walk away with?

Case study length can vary, but a good target length is between 1,000 and 1,500 words. You can always repurpose shorter excerpts as needed.

Here are some prepared questions you can use:

- What prompted you to hire or purchase?
- What hesitations did you have before purchasing?

✈ What surprised you about the process, the service, the people, or the product?

✈ If you had one piece of advice to give to someone in the position of considering this product or service, what would that be?

Case studies should always capture the actual customer's experience, but keep in mind those pain points and audience concerns established during your previous research. If you know from your sales experience or customer research that most of your customers are concerned about getting an ROI, any quotes from your case studies that speak to that point will resonate especially well with other potential clients.

Chapter 11 Action Steps & Takeaways

✈ Determine whether you need any other content on your website beyond just the basics or just the basics and a blog.

✈ If you want to keep it simple, launch with just one lead magnet and follow-up email sequence. You can always build more later.

Outsourcing: Hiring Other Professionals

Now that you know what it takes to create your website copy, you might feel overwhelmed. Remember that getting those core static pages up is a great first achievement.

To Outsource or Keep In-House?

If getting your website copy drafted and published feels like a lot of work, you might consider outsourcing your blogging strategy. Many qualified freelance writers bring a great perspective and SEO knowledge to their work, which frees you up to focus on the work you do best while knowing that your content is published consistently.

CONTENT IS KING

Of course, pros and cons exist to writing your website content on your own. You should consider keeping your copy as an in-house project if:

- You have issues related to compliance because you work with supplements, financial advice, or the law, and you worry that an outside copywriter won't be sensitive to these issues.
- You feel comfortable with your writing skills as long as you have a proven framework for mapping out your website content.
- You're worried about the expense of hiring a content writer or ghostwriter.
- You feel confident you'll be able to meet your self-imposed deadlines for website content.

Hiring a freelance writer to support your editorial blog calendar is best if:

- You have difficulty meeting self-set deadlines.
- You find the writing process overwhelming or slow.
- You're not confident in your writing ability.
- You're not sure you're hitting the right blend of SEO technical writing and voice for your company.
- You've already written some articles and they're not performing well.
- You don't want to continue to invest the time to stay up-to-date on SEO.

Hiring an outside writer is one way to know that the end product is in line with best practices for content marketing. However, there's an art and a science to hiring freelance content writers, and you may not get it right the first time around.

Some people feel perfectly confident in writing their own website content. But if that's not you, that's OK, too. If you don't have the time, capacity, or interest, you can outsource this work.

Anyone can get consumed by perfectionism when thinking about getting a website up. If you're the main writer, you may question yourself. Or you may not feel qualified to judge copy created by a freelancer. Any of that will delay your project and your publish date. This is a dangerous game to play, because every day that goes by without launching your site means missed opportunities.

One of the only ways to gain confidence with the practice of writing is to do it over and over. For aspiring freelance website content creators who are reading this book to improve craft, you'll find that you get better at creating content over time. The process of writing, receiving revisions from clients, and learning more about trends and the best ways to reach an audience will all help you get better at what you do. But for someone who is attempting to create their first finished writing project in the form of a website, the potential for getting stuck in your own head is quite high. That's another reason to hire a freelance website content creator. They've done all the hard work of learning the craft. Rather than just hiring a writer, you're paying for all the months or years of experience they bring to the table.

If you've never hired content writers, my goal here is to save you all the headaches and give you all my ninja tricks for finding the right people for your team, and to teach you how to set them up appropriately so you get the well-written content you need delivered on time. These streamlined systems and my favorite hacks for identifying appropriate content writers will enable you to outsource your content writing projects so that you can focus on other things, knowing your content is being created and produced up to your quality standards.

In this chapter, you'll learn the tricks I use to identify whether someone is the right fit. I'll also share some of the testing tools I use to establish my base team of freelance writers and how to handle common challenges and problems. I look forward to teaching you how to hire content writers so you get the most out of your investment in a freelance professional.

Do You Really Need Outside Writers?

My clients aren't hiring me because they don't know how to write. They're attorneys. They're very intelligent, and they know what they're doing. They might not know how to write for SEO purposes, but they know how to write. However, they recognize that they don't have much time or that this activity does not lead to direct revenue. They generate money by working with clients and winning cases, not writing blog posts or social media updates. Yet they recognize that it's an important component of their marketing strategy, and that's why they outsource it to me. To begin the whole outsourcing journey of working with content writers, you have to understand that you're not hiring someone because you can't do it yourself. You may be able to do it yourself. However, it may be better to hire somebody who understands marketing, writing for the web, or writing for whatever printed materials you have. Outsourcing to experienced professionals can make your life much easier when you do it properly.

You might initially think you don't need to hire outside content writers to increase your business. You might think you can handle content writing on your own. And that's certainly true if you have a background in creating content for the web and you know what your customers are looking for. But you may want to consider outsourcing for other reasons. First of all, it allows you to have a consistent content strategy.

One of the most common reasons people fall off with their content marketing strategy is they're just not able to keep up with it. But when you hire outside content writers to handle this for you, it ensures that you meet deadlines and that you produce content on a regular basis. Now, this works really well when you have somebody who understands your publishing schedule. You may still have to do some work in putting together an editorial calendar. But overall, it allows you to be much more consistent, and that has a lot of benefits for your business, not just with targeting customers but also with SEO. Taking this off your plate also gives you more time. Writing can be extremely time-consuming. Even for an experienced writer, you have to research topics, come up with good ideas, draft posts, and edit them.

While it's important to have a content marketing strategy, your work might not actually be translating to sales. In that case, outsourcing writing to somebody else gives you time to focus on sales, while still maintaining that fresh, high-quality content on your site. When the work created by a team of content writers is optimized properly, it provides more leads on your website.

And finally, hiring a content writer who has experience in the field allows you to tap into working with industry pros who know the ins and outs of the business. That way you're getting high-quality content produced on a regular basis, by somebody who understands the terminology and the jargon of your industry.

Avoid Mistakes in Outsourcing Content

Unfortunately, a lot of people make mistakes when they hire writers for a content marketing team or a content development team. I can help you avoid some of these mistakes.

Not Paying the Right Amount

The first hiring mistake people make is paying too little. There's no doubt that everybody has a budget and it makes sense to stay within a price range. But it's still important to remember that you get what you pay for. If you pay too little, you will deal with more difficult freelancers. They might not pay as much attention to editing, or they might not have the background needed to produce the content. Because they're not being paid adequately, the writers may not prioritize your project.

I once worked on a project where the writers were completely underpaid, and we didn't have the budget we needed to pull off the job. It created a lot of headaches for everybody in the process, including the editor and me, the project manager. We were constantly hounding people to turn in their work and to follow the guidelines, and it generally just created way too much work. I was constantly pushing the client to raise the rates because it generated so much extra work, and it wasn't actually saving the client money. They ended up paying the editor and me more to fix everything.

Prioritizing Price over Quality

Another mistake a lot of people make in terms of pricing is they prioritize price over quality. They will hire somebody who has the cheapest possible rate, because they think "Wow, this person's offering to do it for this really low price. I can get this project off my plate and not have to worry about it."

And then what usually happens is the quality of the work is very low, it's not turned in on time or at all, or it doesn't follow any of your guidelines and pretty much ends up being useless. That's really frustrating. When you outsource writing, always focus on quality, because quality is what serves your business's multiple channels. It's what connects with your audience. It is what helps boost your SEO. Sometimes quality work costs more, but prioritizing price over quality can be a huge mistake.

Not Using Paid Tests or Writing Samples

Not everyone will be the right fit for your project. It's best to see how a potential freelancer works when you start the project, before you get in too deep. I recommend that everyone who plans to hire a freelance writer does so by requesting a paid sample or a paid test. It's unreasonable to ask a content writer to submit free work to you beyond the work samples they have created for the purpose of marketing themselves. Giving a small paid test to your top couple of candidates allows you to see who actually has the chops to be on your writing team.

It also provides a best-case scenario of what the experience of working with a particular writer will look like. Some writers won't follow your instructions or write to your quality standards, and still others will do really well and end up being hired on the project full time.

Not Creating and Enforcing Clear Guidelines

You need to have clear guidelines for your writers to follow. And then you have to back that up. For example, if your freelancers turn things in late for a couple of weeks or they turn in material that is plagiarized or poorly written and you let it slide, it will be really hard to change that standard later on.

However, if your guidelines at the beginning clearly specify that an invoice won't get paid if any part of the work was plagiarized, or that if you or your team have to do more than 20 minutes of revisions on a five-page paper it will be returned to the writer for fixing, that raises the stakes. Writers know exactly what they're responsible for. They can't argue they didn't know those rules. So when you put together guidelines, you need to have not only the guidelines but also the consequences of not following them, as well as your process for review and when writers can expect to hear from you. Having these systems in place can help minimize your headaches when outsourcing content.

Not Knowing What You're Looking For

One big reason a lot of people struggle with hiring writers is they don't know enough about what they're looking for. Perhaps you heard in an industry networking event that you need to be blogging, for example, but you don't really know what kind of writer you need. Does it need to be someone who has a professional background in writing? Or does it need to be somebody in your industry? How long should these blogs be? What is the purpose of these blogs? Are they being marketed for SEO? What do you need to know about keywords? It seems like a lot of barriers to entry exist here.

Not knowing enough about what you're looking for is a problem. Be clear, for example, if you want someone who is self-directed or someone who prefers receiving feedback through multiple rounds of revision.

Not Developing Systems for Onboarding Writers

Another reason people struggle with hiring content writers is because they have an inadequate system for handling the workflow or invoicing.

If that's the case, business owners quickly realize they're in over their head with administrative work. This is particularly true if you're managing a large team of writers. You've got to have a system for how materials will be submitted. And as we mentioned earlier, you need guidelines and rules about due dates, revisions, and what happens when work doesn't meet your standards. You also need systems for invoicing. If you don't have these systems, everything will become chaotic very quickly.

That's true even if you're only outsourcing to one person. If dealing with administrative aspects reaches the point that you're not benefitting from the time savings of working with someone, you will end up frustrated. The good thing is you can avoid all these problems. Many writers are familiar with why you might be publishing content. If they are experienced with this kind of work, they can help you develop strategies and tactics to improve your systems for administrative tasks.

Hiring Freelance Writers: What to Expect

In my nine years as a digital project manager and freelance writer, I have worked with hundreds of writers.

What you'll get in this section is all my best tips for building a content writing team, how to work with people, how to identify whether a potential writer is the right fit, and then how to deal with problems because they inevitably will emerge. I've seen both the good and the bad as it relates to content writers. I like to joke with people that when you identify 10 writers to work on a project, it's almost guaranteed that two of them will completely disappear. That's even after you've offered them a paid writing assignment. Writers unfortunately have a reputation for flaking out. However, amazing content writers are out there, too—people who can help you with your SEO, blogs, ebooks, white papers, emails, newsletters, or any other type of written content you need. You just have to know how to find them and how to work with them effectively.

Freelancers Are Not Just Other Employees

Freelancers are quite different from traditional employees. And as the person managing a digital team or hiring someone on a contract basis, you'll need to understand how content writers like to work, so you can set up the project as effectively as possible.

A contracted writer is not your employee, so don't treat them like one. Freelancers have to be able to call the shots on how and when they do their work. If you try to set specific working hours for your contractor, for instance, you're treating them like an employee.

If you treat them as an employee, the situation is more like an employee-employer relationship. This means you could be responsible for things under the Fair Labor Standards Act in the United States. It can generate a lot of concerns, but you're better off speaking with an experienced employment or business lawyer first to make sure the system you have set up and the foundation of the relationship match the legal parameters.

Even if you're careful, it's easy to end up in a situation where you start treating a contracted person as an employee. And aside from the legal ramifications, freelancers hate being treated like employees.

Do not expect a contractor to return your email within five minutes. Do not expect them to be available at all hours of the day for a phone call. Freelancers often work with 10 to 20 clients at once. If you are the annoying client who calls them often, they will not get back to you, they will find it difficult to work with you, and they will ultimately end that relationship. Do not treat someone as though they are your employee. They are a freelancer, and they work with many people. Be sensitive to that and let them work on their own schedule.

That usually means you provide a submission deadline and detailed guidelines, but then you leave them alone to do the work on their own time and in their own way.

Many people hiring freelancers for the first time are concerned about being taken for a ride. They might be worried about a freelancer ghosting them or failing to follow through with deadlines.

I learned most of the important lessons around hiring freelancers when I managed a team of over 20 writers. During that time, we created more than 400 blog posts a month. I learned so much about what it took to hire them, train them, and support them. I also learned a lot about the administrative work that goes on behind the scenes. Whether you're hiring a writer for the one-time process of creating your website or you're looking to build a team to create your blog content on a regular basis, you need to understand the benefits of setting up a system from the beginning.

One mistake you want to avoid in this process is assuming it cannot be done unless you do it all yourself. It is very common to have a bad experience with a writer and to use that to write off the opportunity to outsource your content altogether. Don't do that. You can effectively use other writers, but you need to hire the right person and it's possible you won't find them the first time around.

The main reason you're probably even thinking about outsourcing in the first place is because plenty of business owners don't want to write, or they're not confident in their writing skills. They don't like doing it. They're not making money doing it. So they'd rather focus on revenue-generating activities. Perhaps you don't even have the time to write. This is why you should hire an experienced professional. Plenty of people hesitate on outsourcing writing because they think "Well, I should be able to do it myself." That's a reasonable thought to have. However, if writing materials is not making you money, it's not really an activity that's worth your time.

Hiring a Content Strategist or a Content Writer: What to Know

The truth is there is definitely an art form to outsourcing content and some key considerations to keep in the back of your mind as you navigate this process. Know that you cannot pass off content strategy, creation, or planning to just any person, because you will need experts at every step of the process, from mapping out your website structure to planning your editorial calendar to developing your social media to help you grow your following to content writing to editing to ensure your content is all appropriately created and produced.

If you are concerned about someone capturing your voice or the complexity of your industry, hire an experienced professional who has knowledge and a background in that industry. You can even hire someone to help you plan your content strategy. A content strategist plans and architects all the content you create, and then those individual assignments might be completed by a separate freelance writer or content writer.

For example, if you work in the health and wellness field, seek out someone who not only has excellent content marketing skills and is receptive to feedback, but a writer with extensive experience in the health and wellness field who will require a shorter learning curve and hopefully fewer edits. A knowledgeable writer who has been in your industry for some time is more likely to get your content right the first time around. They will be sensitive to any unique industry concerns and able to walk the fine line between sharing high-level professional information and connecting with a general audience. I have worked with too many companies who attempt to save money by working with inexperienced writers or writers who don't have an industry background. This almost always backfires and means you end up spending the money on creating the content twice—once on the inexperienced writer and then on either paying a team member or an external editor to fix it or hiring an experienced content writer who starts again from scratch.

What to Look for in a Freelance Writer

You should look for several specifics when outsourcing content writing. Seeing someone's finished work is a great way to get a read on their overall style, but certain characteristics of a freelancer are important, too.

Experience

First of all, somebody who has experience is a great place to start. In an ideal world, your freelancer has experience. That said, there's nothing wrong with finding somebody who has raw talent and drive and then training them to be a part of your content team. In fact, if you hire somebody who's too experienced, they may not have the time for your team. They may be fully booked, or other clients may be demanding their time. But remember, everyone has to start somewhere. I'm forever grateful for the people who gave me my first experience as a freelance writer. I'd never been paid to write for anyone else before.

The freelance writing market has exploded in recent years, which means it can be difficult to find the right person to craft your content. You're looking for someone who has appropriate experience, either on the job, in a volunteer position, or as a content writer. Many talented writers are new to the world of working freelance but might have worked in-house for years, and their experience is definitely enough to service your needs. One of the most important ways to narrow down this field is to review writing samples carefully. We'll cover that more comprehensively in a minute.

Passion and Interest

Second, seek out a writer who has either a passion for writing, an interest or background in your field, or both. Interest in the project itself should always count as a plus for a potential freelance writer. If they're not even remotely interested in working on the project, or you can tell from an initial phone conversation that it's just not up their alley, that will probably be reflected in the work they submit. Interest isn't essential for hiring a content writer, but it's definitely beneficial.

Reliability

Reliability is probably one of the most important traits of a freelancer. You need to be able to communicate with this person easily and they should also be reliable. As I said earlier, busier freelancers can't and won't reply to emails immediately, but they do need to be in regular contact and meet the deadlines you set.

If you have tighter deadlines, reliability and communication may turn out to be even more important. You may need to count on this person to push out your blog posts or other content in quick intervals.

Somebody who has a track record of meeting deadlines and serving other clients successfully can be really valuable for you. It's not always possible to see a freelance writer's background in terms of reputation and feedback. However, you can check places like LinkedIn or an Upwork

HEAR FROM THE EXPERTS
EXPERT: GOGI GREWAL

Background: I've been writing for the better part of a decade, and I have been running my own copywriting business for a year. My background is in health communication, which translates quite well to copywriting.

Listening skills are something you don't hear discussed that much when it comes to copywriting. Listening is actually such a crucial piece of writing website copy. During your kickoff call, a freelance writer needs to really hear what the client is telling them. That means asking the right questions, recording everything in detail, *and* reading between the lines. Some clients are good at explaining what they want and don't want. Others are not so great at expressing themselves (and it makes sense these people would hire a writer to do this for them)! I start every project with a list of questions that I use to fill in my own creative brief for a website project. I write down the goal of the website (what are the primary and secondary actions you want the reader to take?), the target audience, the emotions I want the copy to evoke, and what the brand would be like if it were a person.

profile to find out whether other people have worked with them. Ideally, a freelance writer should also have testimonials posted on their website.

I recommend looking into people's testimonials and background information, because that's one of the most powerful ways to decide whether you want to work with someone. In most cases, writers don't have references you can check. Another client's words and individual experience are likely to be honest, because if the client had a bad experience, they won't provide a testimonial at all. So take those seriously. If you can, always check for client feedback and a freelancer's general reputation.

Someone Who Takes Directions Well

Look for a freelance writer who is knowledgeable about taking directions. Directions are a two-way street, and they are one of the reasons most relationships between freelancers and clients fall apart. Contracted writers love it when a client gives clear directions. But they also hate being told

HEAR FROM THE EXPERTS
EXPERT: VANESSA K. GREEN

Background: Copywriter for eight years. I have 15 years of writing experience. I am a trained journalist and was an editor for seven years before moving into marketing.

By far the most useful thing I've done when writing website copy for my clients is talk to them. I interview them for one to two hours, depending on how much content will be on the website. I ask them questions about their goals and objectives, their biggest challenges, their target audience, and why they do what they do. The insights I gain from these conversations are truly invaluable and make the copy so much more compelling. Most business owners have all this incredibly valuable knowledge about their business in their head, and they just need someone to ask the right questions to get it out of them. This collaboration is what makes the words on their website sing. And it's made me a better listener, a stronger writer, and a much more persuasive storyteller.

their work isn't on par if no guidelines were given. If a freelance writer spends four hours working on a piece for you and submits it, and then you come back and say this isn't what you were looking for, then everyone gets frustrated.

Again, if no guidelines were given, the freelancer had no reason to believe they needed to do anything other than what they did. It's not fair to try to hold somebody accountable to something you didn't provide upfront.

How to Evaluate Freelance Writing Samples

Although this will look different for every single person hiring content writers, I want to walk you through how I evaluate a potential writing sample.

First of all, anyone who submits their work to you for consideration should submit very high-quality work samples. But it's a myth to believe those samples need to be exactly aligned with what you're looking for. For example, let's say you're hiring someone to write a short ebook, and all they have are blog posts or articles for newsletters. That doesn't mean you should rule them out simply because they don't have the exact type of content you're looking for.

Talent is something I look for every time I hire content writers. Talent is far more important than any other aspect of hiring a content writer. Of course you want reliability and an effort to follow your guidelines. But that basic writing ability is essential. We're not necessarily looking for deep knowledge of your industry, unless you're working in a technical industry, such as medical, legal, technology, software, or apps.

Outside of those use cases, you want general writing ability and an ability to do research. I don't spend a tremendous amount of time evaluating writing samples. I judge people very quickly. When you're evaluating multiple people at the same time, you don't have the luxury of looking at every single one of them for 20 or 30 minutes to decide if they're the right fit.

When it comes to SEO knowledge and overall writing ability, you don't need to be a master yourself, but you do need enough basic ability to spot errors in someone else's writing samples. This will help you determine whether you've found the right person to work with your company.

One of the hardest things to change about a writer's work is their underlying style. If you read someone's work sample and aren't impressed or feel that their work is unclear, that it's poorly organized, or that sentences are too long, you'll end up frustrated with the work they submit to you, too. Even if you do bring them onboard, you'll probably end up doing a lot of editing and giving feedback. That might not be worth it. So always review writing samples first to make sure you appreciate their basic style.

Because it can be hard to get someone to adjust their writing style (especially if they've been writing for a long time) and because you don't want to spend too much time training or educating them on what you expect, read through their writing samples carefully.

What you can do is take raw writing ability and create clear guidelines for somebody to follow through on. That means you need to be able to evaluate their writing relatively quickly. If you have specific requirements about how long a paragraph can be, how many subheads need to be used, keyword density, or how the project should be turned in, all of that needs to be listed in your writing guidelines.

Questions to ask as you read through writing samples:

- Do they use grammar properly?
- Are the sentences too short or too long?
- Does this piece flow nicely?
- Have they broken up the text with subheads or visuals so that it's easier to read?

Chapter 12 Action Steps & Takeaways

- Decide: Do you need to hire outside writers for support with your ongoing content marketing?
- If you need outside help, determine how you'll hire people.
- Do you need someone in-house?
- Use test projects to hire the right people.

Final Thoughts

Getting your website launched is a huge achievement, and you don't need to have everything perfect at the time you launch. Simply getting your website up and running with a few pages of strong copy and good design is worth celebrating. Remember, you can always revisit the content marketing strategy material referenced in this book to help you decide how content marketing strategy fits your goals. Your website will continue to be a core of your business and a place to drive traffic, but you might alter the ways in which people get there and find you.

Three Essential Tips to Keep in Mind as You Write

Now it's time for your next steps. If you have an existing website, this is a perfect opportunity to go through your site and conduct an audit. Look at the data you've gathered from places like Hotjar and Google Analytics to see which pages on your site are performing well and which ones might not be worth the continued effort to keep up-to-date.

Your website copy is a living project. It's something you should come back to over time. To help you do that, here are a few of the most important lessons to remember as you craft your site:

1: Always Listen to Your Customer

Your current or prospective clients should drive the way you design your website and the content you put on it. Over time, you'll get valuable metrics you can return to, such as which pages have the highest number of visits or lead to the best action steps of contacting you or signing up for your email newsletter. Use what you learn about your audience both on the site and in customer interviews or testimonials to continually revisit your content marketing.

2: Decide What You Do and Don't Stand For

Earlier in this book you worked on your brand values. Continue to revisit those, as they may evolve over time. Knowing what you want to get across to your prospective clients and readers is important, especially if your company grows. If you're a solopreneur right now, you might write all the website content yourself. But if your company grows and you use freelancers or employees to help tell the story of your company, you'll need to ensure a consistent voice. Knowing your brand values and editorial guidelines will help you with those goals.

3: You Don't Have to Do It Alone

There's a lot of power in knowing what you want to achieve with your website. There's also a lot of power in knowing what to look for in your team members, be they actual employee hires or freelancers. At the end of the day, it's your site and your business or organization, so you need to know best practices to put the final polish on your website and other content. But the good news is that even though a lot goes into content marketing and your website, you can hire plenty of help to assist you with getting a great final result.

About the Author

Laura Briggs is a freelance writer, digital marketing strategist, three-time TEDx speaker, and the author of five books: *Start Your Own Freelance Writing Business, The Six-Figure Freelancer, How to Become a Virtual Assistant, Remote Work for Military Spouses,* and *Content Is King.*

A former seventh-grade teacher, she began working as a freelance content and copywriter in 2012. At the time, she had no formal training in writing or publishing. Laura's writing business followed her through numerous moves for her husband's U.S. Navy career.

Self-taught and motivated by what captures reader and search engine attention simultaneously, she's also worked as a marketing director and has hosted four different podcasts. She's been featured as a guest expert at more than a dozen conferences and on over 150 podcast episodes around the world.

Since getting her start, she's served over 450 clients all over the world, helping everyone from solopreneurs to Fortune 500 companies define and implement their content strategy.

Laura's first book with Entrepreneur, *Start Your Own Freelance Writing Business*, received the 2019 Author Elite Awards "Best in Business" prize. In 2022, Laura was recognized as a "Top 40 Under 40" by the *Illinois Times* and *Springfield Business Journal*.

Laura earned a bachelor's degree in economics and political science from Randolph-Macon Woman's College and a master's degree in political science from Virginia Tech. She's currently completing the coursework for her doctorate in business administration.

Laura has volunteered extensively in the field of domestic violence awareness and prevention and received the Frank Beamer Community Service Award, the Virginia Tech Woman in Leadership Award, and the Virginia Tech Graduate School Service Excellence Award for her work in that area. She currently volunteers as the executive director for Operation Freelance, a nonprofit providing free entrepreneurship training for military spouses aspiring to start their own freelance business.

Laura credits having the courage to start a career as a professional writer to a college professor who suggested she switch her major to English (she didn't, but she thanks Dr. Stiffler nonetheless) and her early mentors, Dr. Craig Leonard Brians and Yuwanda Black. Although both Craig and Yuwanda have since passed away, Laura remains grateful for their insights and votes of confidence to give this whole writing thing a try and to ultimately quit her day job.

Today, she lives with a menagerie of animals and her husband in central Illinois.

Index

Note: Page numbers in *italic* type followed by the letter *f* refer to pages that contain figures.

A

about pages, design and content for, 22, 77–79

accessibility, website, 5, 53

analytics, 139

audience personas, 41–45. *See also* buyer personas

authoritative organizations for content ideas, 130–131

avatars, 41, 72. *See also* buyer personas

awareness stage of funnels, 66

B

backlinks, 99–101

banners, 18–19

benefits vs. features, 142–145

black hat SEO techniques, 101–102. *See also* search engine optimization

blogging, 113–139

about blogs and blogging, 24–25, 113–115

analytics for improving content, 139

bounce rate in, 138–139

categories and tags in posts, 137

core content, 127–129
editorial calendars for, 117–120
generic vs. specific content, 134–135
headlines and titles for blogs, 121–123
images in, 116–117
infographics in, 117
keywords in, 118–119
linking basics, 125–126
organizing your ideas in planning posts, 133–134
outsourcing, 121
repurposing content, 137–138
routines for, 120–121
SEO considerations in posts, 135–136
sources for additional content ideas, 130–133
strategies for, 115–116
talking to more than one reader, 124
target audience for, 130
thinking like readers when creating content, 136–137
what makes good posts, 116
what to post, 123–124
Boller, Rachel C., 42
bounce rate, 138–139
brain traffic model, 106–107
brand credibility, 5
brand editorial guidelines, 53–59, 172
brand values, 35, *36f*, 172
brand visibility, 6–7
Building a StoryBrand (Miller), 12, 62
business goals, 107
buyer journeys, 61–67
buyer personas, 33, 41–45, 64–65. *See also* ideal customers

C

calls to action, 125
Canva, 117, 138
case studies, 150–153
categories, 137
Clearscope, 97
clickbait, 121
client pain points, 55–56
company terms pages, 28
content creation vs. curation, 108–109
content marketing defined, 105
content marketing strategies, 103–111
content roadmaps, 28–29
content strategies. *See also* blogging about, 103–105
analytics for improving content, 139
bounce rate and, 138–139
business goals and, 107
components of, 106
content creation vs. curation, 108–109
content marketing vs., 105–106
content production resources, 109–110
content workflow, 110–111
definition, 105
KPIs and, 107–108
marketing goals and, 106–107
repurposing content, 137–138
target audience and, 35–37, 41–45, 107, 108, 130, 132–133
content strategists, hiring, 162–164. *See also* outsourcing
content workflow, 110–111
contracting writers and strategists, 155–169
about, 162–164

mistakes to avoid, 159–161
pros and cons, 155–159
what skills and experience to look
for, 164–168
overselling results, 52

P

page rank, 87–90, 92–93
performance indicators, 107–108
plagiarism, 49
pop-ups, 139
privacy policy pages, 28
product pages, 27
proofreading and editing, 50, 80–81,
81f, 96
purchase decision phase of funnels,
66–67

Q

quality vs. quantity of content, 52–53

R

Rafeek, Rushda, 11
Ragland, Amy, 71–72
ranking, 87–90, 92–93
reader-centric content, 51
relatability of content, 48
relationship building stage of funnels, 66
repurposing content, 137–138

S

sales pages, 26–27, 141–145
scannable content and SEO, 91
search engine optimization (SEO),
85–102
about, 85–86
backlinks for, 99–101
blogging content for, 135–136
determining what to optimize,
95–96
domain authority and, 89–90

keyword basics for, 91–95
linking mistakes to avoid, 101–
102
page rank and, 87–90, 92–93
scannable content and, 91
searcher intent and, 90–91
tools for, 96–99
value of, 86–87
search engine traffic, 7
searcher intent and SEO, 90–91
Semrush for Keywords, 98–99
services, showcasing, 6
services pages, 23–24, 79–80
short-tail keywords, 92–93
social media for learning about target audiences, 43–45
solo business owner UVPs, 39–40
spelling errors, 50
stock photo sites, 116–117
storytelling, 12–13, 64, 151
subheads, 95
survey research, 43

T

tags, 137
target audiences, 35–37, 41–45, 107,
108, 130, 132–133
template for building content, 70, *71f*
title tags, 95
titles for blogs, 121–123

U

Ubersuggest, 99
unique value propositions (UVPs)
about, 31–33
attracting customers with, 41
determining who you serve,
33–34
examples of, 32–33
finding your ideal customers,
35–37